Between Two Worlds

Gwen Bitti

Between Two Worlds

In loving memory of my parents

And for my grandchildren
Leo, Zachary, Luna, Connor and Rafael
for when they are old enough to read,
they will know that their G'Ma loves and respects her birth
and adopted countries.

Between Two Worlds
ISBN 978 1 76109 537 5
Copyright © text Gwen Bitti 2023

First published 2023 by
GINNINDERRA PRESS
PO Box 3461 Port Adelaide 5015
www.ginninderrapress.com.au

1

Thirty-four years after my family's terrifying flight out of India, here I stand with an Australian passport in hand, Indian-issued tourist visa within. No longer the frightened teenager that I was when I left but a married woman with two adult children and a career.

As I board, there is a rush of emotions – I feel energised returning to the land of my birth but my deceased parents come to mind, along with our complicated escape out of India decades earlier. The fear and concern on that day are still palpable; a warrant having been issued for my father's arrest that could have detained him in India for years, maybe forever. Then it strikes me hard. Is my return foolish? Could the sins of the father be visited on his daughter? Would my parents have approved my return had they still been alive? Despite all we had been through, Daddy perhaps. But Mummy? I shrug. My mother would have reminded me why we had left, and I sense that she would have questioned the reasons for my return. Mummy, like many women in her community, kept her offspring distant from Indian culture. Her constant refrain still echoes in my ears, 'Gwen, you are not Indian, you are Anglo-Indian. We have British heritage.' Her unshakeable belief never waned.

Our family belonged to the Anglo-Indian community of around 800,000 people, crafted by the British in India as a social experiment to create a hybrid community. It was abandoned, along with the country, when the British were expelled from India at Indian Independence.

At Bangkok, my connecting flight to Calcutta, India, is delayed. With time to spare in a hot, airless departure lounge, I am struck hard by a memory of the day in 1971 – older sisters Patricia and Catherine had already migrated to Australia. That left Mary, second eldest sister, who would remain in India, for reasons of her own, the only person at the airport to wish Mummy, Daddy, Nelson, Hannah, Alison and me goodbye as we made our undercover departure out of India. It was clear, if Daddy got out, he could never return to India. The dreaded goal on that day was to make an anonymous and swift exit.

Searing sweat blazes down my neck and back. Is it possible in this age of technology to connect me to my father? This fresh thought frays my nerves and my heart skips beats. The speed at which I do loops of the airport lounge makes it difficult for the wheels on my suitcase to keep up. Each time it topples over, I heave it back into position. My vision blurs, and I wipe away tears with the back of my hand, dry it on my denim skirt.

My mind is weary and my muscles ache. For a few minutes, I am consumed by a desire to forget this whole trip and return to Australia. A nearby lounge looks inviting. I settle back and close my eyes.

Half an hour later, I am startled awake by a blaring airport announcement and jump to attention. Security officials pacing nearby trigger an alarm within. Against my ribcage my heart thumps like a beating drum. I scoop up my handbag and begin a frantic search for my Australian passport. Catching sight of the navy booklet with an Australian symbol on it, I draw it to my chest and feel the blow of my heart against it.

A grey-haired European woman on a nearby seat squints. 'You okay?'

'Yes, thank you. Just tired with all this waiting around.'

'Are you connecting to India?'

'Yes.'

'You nervous?'

'Not at all.' I put on my brave smiling face. 'Can't wait.'

'My first time to India. You?' She muffles, gorging on peanuts.

'Yes, my first time after a long break. I was born there.'

'Oh. I'm Liana. You travelling alone?'

'Yes.' I offer my hand, 'I'm Gwen.'

'I travel on my own, Gwen. You'll be fine.'

'Thank you, I'm sure I will.' I scratch the top of my right eyebrow.

Liana glances at my rolled-up mat. 'You do yoga?'

'I'm a qualified yoga teacher and meditation facilitator.' I pat the top of my mat.

'Are you Hindu?'

I know she means am I Indian but decide to overlook that.

'No, Catholic.' I stand and pull my arms up toward the ceiling, do a few squats.

Liana looks me over, squeezes the top of her head. 'What takes you back to India after all this time?'

'A visit to my homeland.'

Liana leans in towards me and I hear our outbound flight announced. I don't want to continue this conversation and I am swift to wish her farewell.

'Maybe we'll bump into each other again, Gwen?'

In a country of over a billion people, I doubt that there will be a chance meeting again. I smile as she disappears into the crowd. The wild beast in my chest stirs.

On the next plane, I pull out the string of beads which I use to meditate and doze off.

When I awake, many hours have passed. My string of beads dangles from my fingers. Through bleary eyes, I see a man in a turban on the other side of my aisle seat. I nod to acknowledge his presence. He of course takes this as permission to start up a conversation.

'Hello, ma'am. I am Sanjeev, pilot. Were you travelling from Australia and got delayed in Bangkok?' he said in heavily accented English.

With no desire to talk to anyone and guessing the topic of conversation from a man in a turban, if I do decide to talk, the inclination is even less. And who's flying the plane, I wonder.

'Yes, I was.'

'That Ricky Ponting is fantastic,' he crows, twirling the ends of his rich, dark handlebar moustache.

And there it was! Although not remotely interested in cricket, I know that Ricky is the captain of the Australian cricket team and Australia is enjoying a 'golden era' of cricket.

'He sure is.' That concludes my knowledge on cricket. This conversation must change.

'I've never been in the cockpit of a plane,' I blurt, feeling like the biggest fool on earth. Who says that? Also, the world had entered the age of anti-terrorism. Only eighteen months earlier, Australia's Attorney General, Philip Ruddock, had introduced the Anti-terrorism Bill 2004. He described it as '…a Bill to strengthen Australia's counter-terrorism laws in a number of respects…safeguarding all Australians from the scourge of terrorism'.

I am deep in that thought, when I hear the captain.

'Would you like to take a look?'

Being offered the opportunity to view the plane's cockpit was not something that I expected. After floundering for a few moments, I accept the invitation.

'Welcome, ma'am.' The co-pilot's teeth shimmer against his dark skin.

The captain introduces me to a number of instruments on the dashboard. It feels a little crowded in here and I am certain that an in-depth lesson in flying is about to commence, when I experience a sensation similar to an electric shock. As a young child, I had experienced an electric shock – a plug blew up in my hand as I pulled it from the socket. This internal jolt radiates an intense surge of heat.

At this precise moment, the captain announces, 'Ma'am, we have just entered Indian airspace.'

I choke up. The words 'I was born here' barely articulate.

'Whereabouts?'

My voice thick with sentiment, 'Calcutta,' I whisper.

'Oh, that is now Kolkata. It won't be long before we are there.'

It will always be Calcutta to me. Sadness consumes me and slick tears run down my face.

'Thank you, captain. Please excuse me.'

I rush back to my seat and squeeze my eyes tight. A few minutes later, weightlessness abounds and something inexplicable happens – I am outside the plane, flying over Calcutta.

Sunlight dances on the polished marble dome of the grand Victoria Memorial, a building dedicated to Queen Victoria, Empress of India. In all its splendour of pure white marble, rising fifty-six metres high, it sprawls gracefully amidst manicured gardens. Majestic white marble lions guard at the black iron entrance gate.

In the maidan, City Park, directly outside the monument, families play cricket, fly kites. Decorated in vibrant hues of purple, magenta and lime green, plumed horses clip-clop through the dry dirt streets, pulling carriages and creating vapours of dust. Vendors offer their wares to passers-by from wicker baskets, engorged with household items or Indian street snacks – samosas, bhujias, kulfi, puchkas. Bullock carts casually haul coal or bamboo on their daily slog. Gathered around aluminium teapots on pavements, men dressed in traditional dhoti and kurta, loincloth and long shirt, sit on their haunches. From earthenware cups they sip steaming milky chai, saturated with sugar, laced with spiced cardamom and cinnamon.

The city of Calcutta is cradled in a haze of smog, poverty, wealth, overcrowding, beauty and malady. Multitudes of coal fires made in buckets outside shanties are being fanned with cardboard, radiating aromas of cumin, fennel and coriander that reach a crescendo, as if in symphony. Over the Hindus' sacred Hoogly River, the cantilevered Howrah Bridge arches, making way for vessels to ply their trade beneath.

I sense an invisible cloak wrap around me, welcoming me as if I am home and protected. The Newmarket's clock strikes from its blue tower. Its chimes cutting through the city's din. It awakens a poignant bubble deep within – that bursts. Am I English? Indian?

Back in my seat, I tremble with uncertainty, regardless of the answer. Sacredness washes over me and I struggle to make sense of my recent experience. Then, I feel shame that I had never given thanks to my birth country for the enormous privilege that I was given to be born of this spiritual land. With my head held in my hands, 'Thank you, India,' I whisper.

Homesickness comes in waves. I realise that previously I had experienced India through the eyes of adults, but now I stand alone. Raised Anglo-Indian, by British standards, I had never before reflected that India, my birthplace, regardless of my current nationality, possibly has a bearing on who I am today. Flushed with humility as the plane descends on to Indian ground, I vow with determination to find out.

In the Calcutta immigration queue, I stand alongside women, men and children in traditional Indian dress: dhoti, saris, sandals or thongs. In a long denim skirt, white T-shirt and closed black leather shoes, despite my olive skin, I am singled out as – a foreigner.

At the counter, an official opens my passport and smiles broadly. 'Born in Calcutta. Welcome back, ma'am.'

It seems as if the residue memory of British rule still lingers here, even though the British had retreated from India over fifty-five years earlier.

'Thank you for the welcome back,' I say, my voice shuddering.

'Ricky Ponting, Ricky Ponting…what a star, what a star.' The cheerful official chants. Relief washes over me. There is no reference to my departure from India decades ago.

'Yes, he is.'

Indians. Cricket. Almost religion.

The baggage collection area is a sea of men in white turbans, where luggage is tossed and prices for porters haggled. I reach to pull my suitcase off the conveyor belt, but a hand swifter than mine has it in its clutch – bump, bump, bump, off it lifts, onto a concrete floor.

'Stop, stop, that's my luggage.' My voice rises above the hum and chatter.

But it is too late. A porter has placed it high on his turbaned head and is on his way to the exit.

I run alongside. 'Put my luggage down, put it down, put it…'

Out on the kerb, although winter in India, the heat of this December day is intense. It smacks me in the face like a clenched fist.

'Put my luggage down.' My protests are drowned out by cars weaving in rhythm to the sound of their horns. Intoxicated by diesel fumes, and dehydrated, I push my hair off my face and tie it in a knot at the top of my head.

Beggars are upon me – men, women and children with limbs missing, eyes bandaged, hands outstretched. I want to hide from all of this, but there is nowhere to run. My personal space is being invaded by throngs of people moving together. Not an inch of space between us, I am in a shoulder-to-shoulder shuffle on the street.

'Taxi, you want taxi, private car, where you go?' says the porter in his best effort at English. He waves down a taxi, long before my response.

'Transport is organised. I don't need a taxi, put my bag down.'

Thud. My suitcase, a hotcake, is dropped to the kerb and the taxi waved off.

In my bag, I fumble for a water bottle and pour its cool contents over my head.

The porter settles his turban – job over. 'Baksheesh, ma'am.' His hand extends.

I hadn't asked for this service, but payment is required. Elated that my luggage is now in my possession, I place the rupee equivalent of five Australian dollars in his palm. A wide toothless grin tells me I have given far more than was necessary.

Eager to be on my way, I scan the crowd of men holding up roughly torn pieces of cardboard or bold printed names in plastic sleeves – passengers for transfer. Mine isn't there.

After my baksheesh stint, the porter obviously thinks that I am a millionaire. 'Want a limousine?'

'No, I have a car organised. It should be here soon.'

I look at all that surrounds me, and my bulging suitcase. Sorrow overtakes. Do I really need all the possessions in there? With necessities in my handbag, I open my suitcase, remove my toothbrush and then invite those around me to help themselves.

Within minutes, my suitcase is empty and there are requests for chocolate from the children. I didn't have any.

'Chocolate *Nahin hai*.'

The words blurting out shock me. I had not spoken Hindi in all the time I had been away from India, except for a bit of fun in our new country. I then realise that I had been speaking Hindi ever since I stepped off the plane. Overwhelmed with everything happening around me, with nothing left to give from an empty suitcase in hand, and also no ride, I enter a nearby phone booth.

The agent responsible for my transfer apologises, saying a car would arrive soon. A total impossibility in this traffic, and I am quick to learn that everything in India is soon – from a few minutes to months, maybe years. I take the time to buy an Indian telephone SIM – this turns out to be a circus-juggling act, with my phone being managed by every available salesperson. An hour passes before a request for my passport is made for this purchase and my Indian birth in Calcutta noted, which apparently gives me instant clearance.

Out on the pavement, a white Datsun pulls up. The driver leans out of its window, waving a jagged piece of cardboard – 'Mrs Gwen'. I bundle in.

The ride to Beck Began, the last area in which my family lived before we left India, takes more than an hour. Travelling bumper to bumper gives hawkers the opportunity to run up to the car, tap at the window and peddle their wares.

At a red light, peak-hour traffic grinds to a halt. Engines turn off and drivers get out of their vehicles, talk and light up cigarettes. My driver cautions me to keep the windows up as he alights. Pedestrians laden with bundles containing anything from food to equipment carried on their heads or backs, race in between the traffic to cross the road. Cows with no urgency zigzag through the crowds.

The car is directly across from Mullick bazaar, outside the Lower Circular Road Cemetery. Its iron rails are rust-ridden and dried weeds graze through the crumbled tombstones. In memory of lost family and friends, I make the sign of the cross. Open-air stalls at the marketplace display everyday clothing and soft toys strung from bamboo scaffolding eight or ten feet high. Below them are plastic buckets, metal and plastic containers, brooms and knick-knacks. Spices in mounds of yellow, orange and brown, each spiralling up to a point. Gunnysacks bulge with fresh ginger root and pungent cloves. With the traffic at a standstill, there is a continual knock at the car window, 'Drink, ma'am, nice sequin elephant, peanuts…?'

Each time, although not uninterested, I look away. If I wind the window down, I will be mobbed. Also, I have nothing to give them. It's best to distance myself from what surrounds me.

My legs ache and I long to do a yoga posture. I grapple at my yoga mat yearning for a space to roll it out. Then it strikes me: when I lived in India, we never did yoga. The most I knew of it was on the rare occasion that my father had mentioned it in passing. Now, I understand that he possibly had been practising yoga for years – I had seen him levitate, but then I didn't recognise it for what it was. Through my yoga studies in Australia, I knew that for him to be at that stage, he would have been highly evolved and practising yoga for a long time. Unlike the West, where focus is often on the physical side of yoga alone, the East has always been conscious that yoga is about the mind and body and that asana, physical postures, are only one limb of the eight-limbed path of yoga by which we are able to reach samadhi, bliss.

The traffic lights turn to green, but everything remains stationary. It is as if the city is being held in temporary suspension, affording me a moment to reflect on its sights and sounds. These reflections are interspersed by memories of the past with less traffic and fewer people. Now that I am older, everything appears much smaller.

Drivers gradually butt out *bidis*, pure tobacco leaf cigarettes, and take a leisurely stroll back to their vehicles. The slow creep of traffic continues and we make a right turn at a roundabout, when the driver appoints himself as my personal Calcutta guide.

'Park Circus Depot, ma'am,' he says, in his best English accented in Hindi, signalling to an open gate.

A tram rattles out, heads in the opposite direction. So many times,

I had entered and left that depot, meeting friends and riding someplace together.

I wind down the window to acclimatise; the air is thick with smog and grit. The circular botanical garden that once lay in front of the depot is now a dust bowl.

I hear the driver singsong, 'Christ the King Church, ma'am,' rolling the 'Ch' in Christ.

I look up at the faded blue and white statue of Jesus outside the church with his solemn, tired face. Thinking about all that I had passed on the way, my heart melts.

I had expected to be brimming with joy, returning to a familiar locality and staying with Diana who I had known as a child. Instead, with glazed eyes, I am witness to a mass of jumbled bricks and concrete fragments that were once footpaths, now clumped together. The homeless filling and spilling into the street from every available nook and cranny – building entrances, stairwells, under awnings… Greying dhoti bundles piled up like the leaning tower of Pisa, threaten to collapse. Cooking utensils poke through grubby and faded, hole-ridden blankets. Pet dogs and monkeys secured to poles or stacks of bricks with frayed ropes. There are no water vessels for them. My mind takes a walk – these were once tidy, gated premises that graced the streets with poise. Did I really once live here? Shaken, I dab humidity off my face and neck. I hear the wail of a police siren drawing closer. My heartbeat vibrates in my ears. Are they here for me? I wrap a scarf around my head and face, exposing only my eyes.

The police car is parallel to the car that I am travelling in. A policeman motions to the driver to pull over. I pray to be invisible. The police car pulls in at the nearest kerb and my driver pulls up behind it.

The driver turns to me and says, 'Ma'am.'

I startle and jump a little out of my seat. The blood in my head is pumping with the terror of being thrown into the back of a police car and taken to the authorities to be questioned about my father. I compose myself. 'Yes, driver.'

'The police are wanting little bribe money.'

I don't question what they want bribe money for. I open my wallet and hand the driver five hundred rupees, the equivalent of ten Australian dollars and say a silent prayer that they will soon be gone. I don't know or care to know anything more about the situation. I tremble as the policeman walks over to us. Nausea rises from my stomach and settles in the pit of my throat. The driver gets out of the car to talk to the policeman and, again, I think about that terrible day all those years ago when my family left India. I see the driver shake the policeman's hand and know the money has been passed. Back in the car, the driver acts as if nothing out of the ordinary has happened. I then realise it is harassment money and the driver is used to being pulled over.

Even so, thoughts of being detained by the police are scrambling through my brain, when the driver's perky voice snaps me out of it.

'I want to go to Australia, ma'am. Can you get me in?'

'Pardon?' I sit upright and straighten my shoulders. Dumbfounded that he has recovered from this ordeal within seconds, while I am still reeling in the aftershock.

He repeats the question and I squirm with embarrassment at the request – the idea that he thinks I have such power. He could not know how difficult that process was for me and my family. Continuing with his request, he elongates each word, elevates the pitch, as if he thinks I have difficulty understanding or have perhaps lost my hearing.

'Cann youu heelp mee geet in-to Au-stra-lia, ma'am?'

'Driver, Australia has an immigration policy. You have to apply. I don't decide who gets in.'

The nerve, thinking I can get him into Australia. Relax, I tell myself. My abruptness towards him embarrasses me, but he doesn't appear to notice as he rushes to explain the turmoil and partial fence cordoning an upcoming area.

'Quest shopping centre coming here, ma'am.'

'What shops will there be?' I try to engage in this unnecessary conversation, in recompense for my previous rudeness to him.

'Gucci, Jimmy Choo…' He rattles off Western world designer shops that will occupy the new centre.

'Luxury shops.' I try to be interested, but my head is spiralling.

'Yes, ma'am, six cinemas, parking, very fine. This, ma'am, was once an electricity substation, now all broken up…'

I then recall the cinnamon-coloured walls that once shut the view of the substation from the street but, to me, the area is no longer recognisable. His words flow like a mechanical recording he has played to tourists numerous times.

The driver takes a left turn and I lose all sense of orientation and wish I could switch off listening to him.

'How long will you stay in Kolkata, ma'am? If you want car, call me any time. Ma'am, your stay in India will be, very, very good. It won't leave your mind. I think you will come back again and again.' He wobbles his head, which is characteristic of Indians, who shake their heads from side to side and could mean yes or no, or both.

I know these scenes will linger in my mind for a long time to come, and I bite hard on my lower lip. At this point, his predictions of my numerous returns don't seem very likely.

Without indicating, the driver pulls into the kerb, near a host of people assembled on the pavement around a *chappakal* – a three feet tall grey metal water pump. Under it, a man in a loincloth is lathering himself; soft clouds of soap swirl around his upper body. With one hand he pumps water, with the other he washes. Beside him, men are shaving, brushing teeth, washing clothes. Queued at the *chappakal*, people smile and chatter to each other. Each one holding buckets, plastic containers or earthenware pots, in which to collect water.

On the same pavement, a woman in a magenta and olive-green nylon sari is preparing what must be the evening meal on a portable gas stove – rolling out saucer-size dough circles on a board, then dry-frying on a metal plate – Indian bread, roti. She stirs the contents of a small brass pot. Beside her, a fishmonger displays his catch of pomfret and tuna on plastic sheets – eyes bulging, fins wriggling. Across from him, outside a mosque, children are at play. Again, I wind the window down a little to attune to the ambience – the density in the air has changed and is laced with the aroma of spices, prattle and loud music.

'Your destination, ma'am.' Abruptly, the engine is switched off.

My palms sweat, 'Can't be. Is, is, this the address I gave you?' With no visible street signs, I am none the wiser.

'Yes, ma'am. I am getting your luggage.'

A wave of threat encircles me, I think about my tourist visa, the police episode earlier, now the unfamiliar surroundings and become paranoid that I am being set up.

'No, don't. Don't get anything out. Just wait.' I phone Diana. 'My driver says it's the address I gave him, your address. Nothing looks familiar.'

'Can you see a post office and opposite it a pink and green mosque?'

'Yes.'

'You are at the correct place. Wait, I'm coming.'

There was no immediate plan for me to go anywhere else. I get out of the car.

'*Accha*, okay, driver, this is the place. You can get my luggage out now. But don't leave yet. Wait until the memsahib comes for me.'

'If that is what you are wanting, ma'am.'

'Yes, it is. *Shukriya*,' I thank him.

'*Dhab?*' A vendor waves a sickle in my face, ready to crack open the top of a coconut for its water, should I want to take up the offer.

I don't.

The *modi*, all-sorts shop, with shoppers crammed at its entrance, proves to be an obstacle course of grain sacks and bottled water. Bugs are drawn to a bare light globe, which dangles from exposed wires trailing across a blue plastic-covered extension. Two timber posts support the entire contraption.

A rounded swarthy figure is walking toward me, roughly five-foot-tall in a blue and white dress, with a dark cardigan draped over it. I don't totally recognise her, but guess it is my hostess, Diana. She peers through rectangular framed glasses; a wave lets me know that I have been spotted.

'You're here. Come, come let us get inside. Noisy out here.'

With the car prepaid, I turn to the driver. '*Shukriya*. Thanks, you can go now.'

'Ma'am, a little baksheesh, please ma'am.'

Have I not just paid his bribe money? I don't want to question that, so I pull some small denomination rupees from my wallet. Unlike the airport porter, I receive a mediocre smile and a head wobble. I take it as a 'yes', and feel pleased that I have probably mastered the correct amount to tip.

'Call me again if you want car.'

'*Accha*, okay.'

Two hundred feet away from the mosque, we enter a narrow passageway. I navigate my empty suitcase in the fading light, over a path of lumpy concrete and stones. To my right, atop a ten-feet-high wall, shards of thick green and brown glass are concreted in, sharp ends pointed upward.

Diana must have caught my glance. 'It is to stop the thieves climbing over the wall.'

Why would they climb over the wall, when there was no gate at the entrance to this property or the one on the other side? Surely, they could easily walk through? My thoughts stall when the *bisti,* water deliveryman, with his full leather water sac, manoeuvres past us. To make way, we squash to one side.

This sets off some sort of urgent trigger for Diana. She leaves me, rushes to her door, undoes a million latches and locks to the steel security door and then again at the main door.

Diana lives at the bottom of a three-storey building of six flats, two on each floor, old but solid, with high ceilings. At its entrance, black marks streak the walls and the electricity meter boxes are a mass of bulging wires. Once inside her flat, she races down a hallway of red polished concrete. Metal clangs together and almost deafens. I follow the mild smell of disinfectant and reach the bathroom. There she stands, hose in hand poised at a metal washtub, amidst six or seven buckets and aluminium basins.

'We only get water pumped twice daily, at six.'

Water gushes out of the hose on cue, and she moves it from container to container as she fills each one.

The kitchen has a faint smell of gas, a double burner portable cooker and utensils in neat piles, covered with *jharans*, tea cloths. In the drawing room, the ceiling is patchy where paint has peeled off. Lime-green paint curls cling to the top of the nine-feet-high walls – cherubs ready to float down. Typical of an Anglo-Indian home, an altar is affixed to the wall, a lighted candle flickers in a blue glass holder below. A solid mahogany dining suite with six chairs occupies a large portion of the room. The table is set with a white damask cloth, a silver teapot, cups and saucers. A matching mahogany showcase is filled with curios, it overlooks three sofas and a centre table. The entire room is odorous of melting wax.

Diana pours Darjeeling tea, stirs in the sugar with a silver spoon. I gift Diana with Australian treats, Tim Tam biscuits, Vegemite, caramel chocolate koalas, blocks of Cadbury dairy milk chocolate and a small souvenir stuffed kangaroo.

'How is all the family in Australia, Gwen?'

'Everyone is very well and successful, thanks for asking, Diana. There have been additions to the family with the many marriages and arrival of grandchildren.'

We discuss each family member individually until Diana is updated with names of the new additions and what everyone is currently doing.

'It is so lovely to hear how well everyone has done. It makes the sacrifice your parents made worthwhile, Gwen.'

I smile and take delicate sips of tea, 'Where have all the Anglo-Indians gone, Diana? I haven't seen any at the airport or on my way to this neighbourhood.'

'In this area, they are few and far between now. The Mussalmans have pushed them all out. The Hindus won't give Mussalmans properties where they have congregated, so they have moved around here. Our Anglo-Indian community is disappearing. There are only small numbers left in India, mostly concentrated here in Calcutta. You know this city now has an Indian name? I prefer to still call it by its English name. There has been a lot of intermarriage, not like before, when an Anglo-Indian marrying an Indian would have been rare, even shameful.'

I recall that Anglo-Indians rarely mixed socially with Indians. 'I see. Pity they've all gone.'

'What brings you back to India, Gwen?'

'I was born here, and left as a teenager, felt it was time to pay my birth land a visit. Be Indian again.'

Diana puts her cup down and stares at me, wide-eyed. 'You are Anglo-Indian, not Indian.'

'I'm Indian, I was born here.'

'Think about what you are saying. Your mummy wouldn't have liked to hear you say that. You are of British descent – Anglo.'

I can tell from Diana's feverish movements she is uncomfortable with this conversation.

'Again, what is it you do in Australia, Gwen?'

Although Diana has lived in India for over seventy years, she still has her English mannerisms, but I suspect she knows fluent Hindi, from the pamphlets on a chair.

Shadows from the overhead fan skim over a Madeira cake.

'I'm an accountant and a writer, but I also teach yoga…meditation.'

'Yoga?' She raises her voice as if it were a life-threatening occupation.

Being Anglo-Indian, her surprise was understandable. Raised as if we were an elite layer within India's people, we learned English nursery rhymes, Shakespeare, a Catholic Latin Mass and the Gospels. Read Enid Blyton, Mark Twain and other English or American classics. But her reaction also struck a chord for me.

'Yes, I've studied their scriptures too. I plan on visiting some major

Hindu religious places, such as Varanasi.' A pang of guilt stabs me in the heart at drawing the line of distinction 'their' segregating the Anglo and Indian.

Diana looks at me with a furrowed forehead. 'Your family don't mind?'

'I don't think so. I have never actually asked their permission, didn't feel the need.'

'What do you intend to see in Calcutta?'

'I want to travel down memory lane, places of my family homes and the like. I'm working on the family tree, so I'll collect documents where possible.'

'Have you many family friends here in India to catch up with?'

'Sadly not. Most of the people we knew have either left India or their whereabouts are unknown. I have the phone number of an old neighbour, Melvyn from when I was a kid and lived in Elliot Road.'

'Come, you must be tired, I'll show you to your room.'

On the way, I am instructed about being careful, where to catch the trams, where to walk, where not to walk…staying out too late.

A red silk carpet runs alongside an Edwardian bed and matching dressing table. Cushions on the red velvet sofa have been freshly plumped. A permanent crucifix is nailed to the wall above the bed.

'Hope you will be comfortable.'

'Thank you, it's more than sufficient.'

'I cannot assist you in the mornings. I supply work lunches for a dozen or more people on a daily basis. They love my potato chops, my speciality. We still love our English fare, but I can also make *panthras*, Indian pancake snacks, curries and other favourites. The *Khana-Coolies*, tiffin-carriers, collect before noon. Do you remember that?'

'Yes, I do remember our home help, I mean ayah, rushing to fill the metal tiffins for collection.' The lunch carriers fill my mind – up to thirty tiffins filled with rice, curries, roti and vegetable dishes, or an English meal, carried and distributed via bicycles. Each one labelled with a system of symbols and colours, denoting where the tiffin is picked up, and the owner's final address – all hand-painted. The lunchtime delivery, never late.

'Would you like nice soup and cutlets for dinner?'

What about curry and chapatti? 'Thank you, Diana, that would be lovely.'

'Be careful when you are out and about, Gwen. You are Anglo-Indian, you know.'

2

The Anglo-Indian community was born in 1911, when the Viceroy and Governor General of India, Lord Harding, officially decreed the offspring of European fathers and Indian mothers as 'Anglo-Indian'. The declaration was then included in the *Government of India Act 1919* and further strengthened in 1935.

The English East India Company had long been trading with India for commercial use of spices. To secure these trading ties, they negotiated with the Dutch and Portuguese, who had settled in India before the 1600s and purchased a strip of coastal land. A harbour and fort were constructed on the site at Fort St George, Madras – modern-day Chennai.

At Fort St George, English men established relationships with the Europeans and Anglo Celtic women by either marrying them or taking them as mistresses.

The British, who for the greater part of their working lives lived in India, occupied most of the senior positions in professional work and government departments or were merchant traders and planters. These long-serving British often referred to themselves as Anglo-Indian. Remaining loyal to the British, they committed themselves to the government and development of India. In doing so, they became less 'British' and more 'Indian'.

For me, entering India again and learning of the intermarriages stirs up thoughts and ideas that I had not considered previously. While Indians and Anglo-Indians worked together, they rarely interacted socially.

India's caste system, since ancient times, divides groups of people into hierarchical categories by classification and also colour in a social structure that entitles each caste to perform specific jobs. Members of higher castes have a higher social status than individuals of a lower caste. This system is especially important in relation to marriage, where traditionally people don't marry outside their own caste.

The highest of the castes, Brahmins, are priests or teachers. Followed by the military class and tradespeople. The lower classes work as child carers, cooks, general housekeepers and chauffeurs. The lowliest of all, Dalits or untouchables, have jobs confined to waste removal and are of such a low caste that they are not permitted to study the earliest sacred Indian literature or even step into the shadow of a higher caste. Within this system, thousands of castes and sub-castes exist. The British Raj during its rule in India reinforced this system and established the categories.

Servants never sat at our tables, or in our drawing rooms, except on the floor. They were not invited to celebrations or to share our meals, regardless of how long they had served the family.

I remembered an old school friend who had a huge crush on an Indian boy and took every possible opportunity to flirt with him in secret. She was forever fearful of her mother's wrath if she was found out. Back then, as children, we never understood the caste system. We simply knew that we were Anglo-Indian and not to socialise with Indians.

For the majority, Anglo-Indian children were constantly drilled that their ancestry was British or European. 'Aluminium' for Anglo-Indian was one of the first learned words in my vocabulary. Anglo-Indians contained socialising, relationships and marriages primarily within their own community. Despite India being their country of birth, many Anglo-Indians never knew or learned the national language, Hindi, fluently.

Many children were privately tutored to read and write Indian languages, which were compulsory subjects at school. Anglo-Indian-only schools discriminated and ignored teaching of outstanding Indians such as Kalidas, considered one of the greatest Indian literary talents of all time. Also neglected was Rabindranath Tagore, a Bengali poet, philosopher, artist, playwright, composer and novelist, who was India's first Nobel laureate, and won the 1913 Nobel Prize for Literature. Tagore's friends included many notable twentieth-century figures such as William Butler Yeats, H.G. Wells, Ezra Pound and Albert Einstein.

Many Anglo-Indians never wanted to be Indian. The way that the Anglo-Indian community aligned itself exclusively with the British and Europeans amuses me now that I am married to an Australian-born Italian. It was not a conscious decision; it was the way it worked out. Though my studies of yoga and Hindu philosophy in Australia came easily to me – almost as if they were at my core waiting to be unravelled – I had never given much consideration to these alignments myself, until that poignant moment that I re-entered India.

Alone in my room at Diana's place, I search my phone list for a domestic airline, and book flights to places interstate that I have planned to visit. I find Melvyn's number and call.

'Melvyn speaking.'

'Hello, Melvyn, it's Gwen, your ex-neighbour from a long time ago. I wrote to you. Did you receive my letter?'

'Gwen, it is lovely to hear your voice. Are you in Kolkata already?

'Yes, I am. I'll have to remember to say Kolkata instead of Calcutta. I'll be in Elliot Road the day after tomorrow. Do you still live there?'

'Can't leave the place. I prefer to call it Calcutta.'

'I know it's a work day for you and wonder what time you get back in the evening?'

'Leave it with me, I will organise something. What time do you expect to be here?'

'I plan on the morning. Perhaps we can catch up then or another day. I'll be in Calcutta for a few weeks.'

The next afternoon, eager to buy Indian clothes for my stay and explore all things Indian, I take a brisk walk to the local market, when I hear my mother's voice, '…in before dark, Gwen'. Now a grown woman with my own family, I think it ridiculous to pay heed to the instructions

I was given in childhood. But my mother was forever protective and had a constant fear of me staying out on my own after sunset. I loved her for the way she looked out for me and kept me close to her. I find it impossible to ignore the echo of her foreboding advice that takes me back to my childhood, and I commit to honouring her and returning home before sunset.

Mummy would also see me as discrediting her by wearing Indian clothes and I choose to ignore that thought. When I lived in India, I never wore Indian clothes. Anglo-Indians had a self-imposed rule, forbidding them to wear Indian attire. They wore British-style clothing, females in jackets, skirts and frocks, males in suits, shirts and ties and casual versions of that dress code.

At the market, the fragrance of spicy chicken and onions being tossed on a skillet and then rolled up in Indian bread, paratha (*kathi-roll*), tantalises. I walk around the market eating one, held in newspaper, when I hear, 'Gwen, Gwen, over here.' The voice is whooping, spiking its way through chicken feathers and the waft of fish smells.

'Hello, Liana, I never expected that I would see you again once we departed Bangkok airport. Are you staying around here?'

'I'm staying at the Mother Teresa place. It's not far from here.'

'I know the place. When my sister, Hannah and I were teenagers, we were regulars on Thursdays for Mass. We also did small jobs for Mother Teresa.'

Liana places her hand on her heart, 'You met Mother Teresa?'

'Yes.'

Liana touches my arm as if some of Mother Teresa's holiness has rubbed off on me.

This city of Calcutta makes me feel as if I belong, but it has nothing to do with me having met Mother Teresa, although it is a privilege and blessing to have been in the living presence of that holy woman.

At a nearby tea wallah, tea vendor, who supplies piping hot milky brew, Liana and I exchange travel plans, which will take us in different directions. Together, we continue our exploration of the market, helping each other with clothes choices. Liana satisfies her curiosity for Indian jewellery, while I revisit past experiences, but only now appreciate all I had missed – handicrafts exclusive to India, handmade trinkets – silver ankle bracelets, sequined fabric elephants and shoulder bags, coir fans, batik scarves and traditional garments. I am deeply engrossed in beaten-tin ornaments when once again, I hear my mother's mantra, '…in before dark'.

With hands laden, I wish Liana well, hasten a goodbye, and race out of the puzzling market light into the glow of a setting sun.

3

On my return, I am keen to tell Diana about my chance meeting with Liana.

'That's nice,' she says and hastens to set the table for dinner.

I lend a hand. The lights flicker and the ceiling fan starts to slow.

'Load shedding. The power will be cut for hours.'

Those words bring back a powerful memory for me. 'How long will it last, Diana?'

'One can never predict, sometimes an hour, sometimes overnight. I will get candles. Still want to be Indian?'

'We experience power cuts in Sydney too, Diana. I was born here, I am Indian.'

In the fading light, I am drawn back to when I was twelve years old.

My mother singled me out one hot summer's afternoon. 'Gwen, we need to talk.' In the drawing room, Mummy sat on a rattan-backed sofa.

Older sisters, Mary and Catherine, had returned from work, happy that their five-and-a-half-day work week was over. Both were readying themselves for the tailor's weekly visit to collect patterns and fabrics for dresses. Following that, they would keep their Saturday afternoon appointments for the hairdresser and beautician.

Nelson and Hannah were born two years apart to the day. They share an uncanny connection; whatever ails one physically is sure to ail the other. That day, they were concocting something mysterious, with flour, water, candles and matches on the tiles of the bathroom floor, which would mean we would all be in some sort of trouble with Mummy by the end of the day. Still, I desperately wanted to be with them, and share in their misfortune.

'Where's Alison?' I asked Mummy, in the hope that she would forget our talk and go in search of the youngest in our family.

But Mummy wasn't being swayed. 'She's playing.'

'Can I go and play with her?' I didn't really want to play with a nine-year-old, but anything was better than a talk with Mummy right now.

'Gwen, I have already told you we need to talk.' Mummy tapped the wide jarrah armrests with her nails, creating a drumming sound. 'Your father gave me this.' She ran her index finger around the circumference of a gold box, as if she were about to conjure up a spell.

'I lined this box with special paper, for protection. The caul you were born with has been stored with the family heirlooms. I thought, when it was appropriate, I would give it to you.'

Mummy opened the lid a little, to show me what she was talking about. But all I got was a glimpse of paper.

'That's nice, Mummy.' I scanned the rest of the room. The Grundig had a few Jim Reeves long-playing records resting on top. Mummy's curio cabinet bulged with ornaments, crystal glasses and her fine china dinner set with twenty-two-carat gold trim; the one she used for dinner parties. The bookshelf laden with Daddy's leather-bound books. The radio beside it hummed faintly with its *Akashvani Calcutta* signature tune, which preceded the news.

'The day after you were born, when your father and I brought you home from the hospital, I laid the caul over the mirror on my dressing table. Nervous at the fact that I knew nothing of such a thing, nor was I able to make sense of it, I prayed to the dear Lord for guidance. We then decided not to mention it to anyone who came to see you after your birth.'

'Is that all, Mummy?'

Mummy obviously didn't hear me. 'When you presented with this at your birth, I was terrified. I thought something attached to your head and face would have restricted your breath, its removal would scar your face, surely it would affect your physical health adversely.'

Back then, I didn't make anything of my mother's remark, but now that it is in my possession, my curiosity is piqued and I wonder, had she ever considered that it might affect me emotionally or spiritually one day?

The tale of my special birth was related to me by my mother. 'You were born in Calcutta's heat, in the middle of May. On the morning of your birth, Ayah didn't bother to pull the curtains back from the windows. The fan's blades creaked from being overworked. Jumadhar, sweeper, had been earlier that morning to wash the floors in an effort to keep the place cool.

'In the drawing room, I sat to pray the rosary. Nana placed a vinegar-soaked cloth on my forehead, to relieve my headache. She told me not to worry about the children, she would take care of everything.

'Halfway through a Hail Mary, I knew that it wouldn't be long before I had to leave for the hospital, so I asked Nana to call Daddy and tell him to hurry, but your grandmother had already taken care of that too. There was load shedding and I prayed that the electricity would not go off now. So often the power was cut without warning for hours at a time.

'Your father came through the door breathless, looking flushed and a shade paler than usual. Although I had given birth five times before, he was still nervous about the impending birth. I was so pleased to see him. Without prompting, he raced into the bedroom and picked up the tan-coloured suitcase.

'The heat sweltered as we walked down the narrow laneway to the main street, where a rickshaw man waited. My white, lace cotton handkerchief was soaking from dabbing my face for only a few minutes.'

I slouched deep into the lounge, began a thorough investigation of the rattan, and tried hard to listen to Mummy, in case she asked a question.

'Ayah ran behind me, offering me water from a thermos and trying to obscure me from Daddy. The servants who lived down the laneway peeped at us. The women hastily pulled their head coverings over their faces because Daddy was with me, and the men kept their heads down in respect for me.'

'My blood curdled when Everard, who lived in a house along the way screeched, "Aunnnntie, Aunnnntie…"'

Mummy screeched it out as if she were now that boy. That was enough to make me sit bolt upright.

'It was heartbreaking to see a grown boy with distant, glassy eyes shake the metal bars on the window of his family's home and call out as if asking for help.'

'Why did he do that, Mummy?' I was astonished that Mummy was so animated.

'Brain damaged at birth.'

We stared at each other briefly.

Mummy shivered and I looked away, sank back into the lounge and started to stick my fingers through the holes in the patterned rattan. A finger got caught in the rattan and I wrenched it out, scraping skin off. I winced in pain, wiped off the trickle of blood that had run down the side of the cushion.

'Are you paying attention, Gwen?'

'Yes, Mummy.' I continued my creative designs and tried to keep up with Mummy's story.

'Opposite Everard's place, a curtain flapped shut, shielding the red-haired Anne who had recently been diagnosed with a deadly disease. The word cancer, then, was feared and rarely uttered. The narrow-minded people of the neighbourhood passed judgement on her, declaring her afflictions as her fate for her unsavoury life. I said a Hail Mary for both sides of the laneway.'

'What is an unsavoury life?'

'You don't need to know that.'

'Why?'

'Because.'

Often that explanation sufficed for the question at hand.

'When we reached the rickshaw in which we would travel to the hospital, rickshaw wallah fastened the suitcase behind the carriage. Your father asked me repeatedly, "Lovie, are you OK?" And, in his Anglo-

Indian/Hindi accent he hurried the rickshaw wallah along. *"Juldi, chullo, chullo."'*

Mummy smirked as she said the words as if she knew how to say them, though I knew she didn't. Mummy and Daddy never knew Hindi, except for a few words that they had learned from the servants. Both came from the south of India and in addition to English knew other dialects, which we children didn't know nor did the servants. With English being the common language that we spoke with our parents, and Hindi or Bengali to the servants, it was sport for us to play off the servants with parents and vice versa to suit our own ends.

'Rickshaw wallah took off like a heat-seeking missile. Dodging traffic, he pounded a metal bell against the wooden rickshaw handle, ting-ting-ting, to warn the cars, scooters, pedestrians, chickens, cows or dogs of his approach, while an overloaded ramshackle passenger tram chugged alongside them.'

Mummy's face turned sad. 'On one side of the street, a beggar woman outside her impoverished home nursed a newborn from her shrivelled breast. She had probably given birth to it there hours earlier. I felt so privileged going to a private nursing home, with a room to myself, and nurses to fuss over me. My heart went out to the woman and her baby, but a short sharp contraction made me wish I was already at my privileged destination.'

I heard laughter in the background and wondered what I was missing out on. 'Mummy, I'll go and play with Alison now,' I said from my sprawled lounge position, and with stealth moved to make my exit.

'Gwen, sit down please, I'm not finished.'

Reluctantly, I squatted on the silk carpet and picked at the threads.

'With a filthy rag for a handkerchief, rickshaw wallah wiped sweat from his neck and brow. The rickshaw's back canvas flap had been removed, and hot gusts blew through. In melody, its wooden wheels gyrated a mechanical clickkkkkk, click, clickkkkk. Rickshaw wallah's thick, parched, cracked bare feet appeared oblivious to the hot melting tar on the streets. His bony, sweaty body glistened in the sunlight.

'The heat overwhelmed me and nausea started to rise into my chest, moments before Madan Street came into view, where the click, click slowed and stopped at 3-A. I saw the large brass sign at the entrance: Avenue Nursing Home. Instantly, it comforted me. And, as if heavenly sent, a wheelchair and two nurses in blue and white cotton saris, with stiff white-winged caps, awaited my arrival.'

Now, Mummy had my undivided attention. These were not things children and adults discussed. I knew that Mummy had drifted off into a space where it was obvious that she had forgotten she was talking to me, a child. I was quick to recognise this golden opportunity to learn about the unspoken happenings in life. I sank back into the rattan lounge.

'I knew there was only a short time now before I would deliver. Aware of the acute pain that would come soon, I accepted that in labour it was a necessary and uncomfortable part of the birth process.'

'What pain in labour, Mummy? What were you going to deliver?'

These were useless questions. I don't believe Mummy even heard me and I had no idea what she was talking about. I returned to making creative new shapes by pushing my fingers through gaps in the rattan. The holes were spread wide open now and they squashed all the smaller holes together in a tight fit. When Mummy looked in my direction with her far-away eyes, I sat up straight, to hide my new rattan shapes.

'Once I saw Doctor Nag, my Indian physician and obstetrician of many years, entering the delivery room, I knew I was in safe hands.'

I thought Mummy said ostracism, but decided it was best not to ask about that or I would be here much longer than need be.

'Dr Nag always greeted me, referring to me as mother. He commented that I was about to give birth to my sixth child. He smiled his usual comforting smile and the light caught a solid gold tooth and it shimmered. His white shirt and pants contrasted against his dark skin and hair. For a man his age, he showed no signs of greying.

'He assured me after an examination that all was perfectly normal. Contractions came in consistent waves. I felt their intensity and knew that I had to push. His voice infiltrated the recess of my brain some place, "Mother, can you do one more push please, one more push?" The sound echoed in my head, as if I were in a void.'

'What did you have to push, Mummy?'

Mummy shifted awkwardly and the drawing room drained of sound, except for the radio programme, *Askashvani Calcutta,* hissing in the corner. Mummy's face drained of colour. 'Doesn't matter. You were born. You didn't cry.'

'I was a good baby.'

'I couldn't see you, but everyone else was staring at you.'

'Why were they staring at me?'

Mummy looked at me, but it was clear to me that she was unaware that I was in the same room as her, yet she responded.

'I did not know. You were not crying. Fear and panic coursed through my body. Anguish took its hold. I experienced the darkness of distress and took refuge in prayer. In a crowded room, in a city bulging with people, I felt alone.'

Mummy scrunched her handkerchief into a ball. 'The doctor's mouth moved, yet the words were unclear in my ears. His face was tense and his hands moved expeditiously. Nurses rallied around. I asked what was wrong but no one answered. Matron Phillips had her gaze firmly fixed on something. Now, I know it was on you. But back then, I felt my breath restrict and my chest tighten. The nurses held my hands, wiped my forehead, and looked at me with pitiful faces, for what I felt was an eternity. I thought the worst, then you cried, and I jerked out of my abyss, my breathing restored in an instant. Matron Phillips held you up and announced: Female child, time of birth twelve forty-five p.m. Eight pounds twelve ounces.'

My mother's face blazed red with embarrassment when she realised that she had imparted all this information to me. At twelve, she would have considered me far too young to hear all of what she had said. I sat as quiet as a snake ready to strike.

'What happened, Mummy?'

As if in Catholic communion, she raised the gold box that she held. 'Dr Nag lifted the membrane for me to see. It is inside this box and is the size of a lady's handkerchief. With his chest puffed up, he carefully placed the membrane on a nearby table that was lined with a sterile cloth and identified it as a "caul" and said that you were a special girl to be born with it.

'After closer inspection, he smiled, exposing his gold tooth once again, as if it were deliberate, to emphasise preciousness. "Mother, this is a rare birth, I have heard of such a birth before." His head, a pendulum swinging, yes, no, yes, no. "But I have never encountered this phenomenon. This child is going to be very lucky. She will never want, but life will not always be easy for her. She will have extrasensory ability to see beyond the ordinary." His bushy, black eyebrows lifted and danced. "This membrane, like a veil, covered her entire face. I had to put my fingers under it and lift it off her face, so that she could breathe. I did not cause dam-age to your bay-bee or her veil." Triumph now his middle name, he smiled. "I will see you after you take some rest and I will tell you more about the caul. We will let Sir know that his fifth daughter is a special girl."

'He continued to talk but, once you were in my arms, I never heard what else he had to say. I counted your fingers and toes, checked your head for scars, but there were none. I was allowed to hold you for a few minutes and then the nurses took over. They gave me a back rub, followed by a cup of tea.'

The timing for a cup of tea was perfect, and I called Ayah. Together with our tea, she brought gulab jamuns. The milk-solid dessert, made into bite-size balls, deep-fried then soaked in sugary syrup, laced with rose water, was the sweetest treat she could offer right now. Mummy was deep in thought as we ate and drank.

I put my cup down. I could hear laughter in the background and wanted to join in. I tiptoed to the door. 'I'll go and find Alison.'

'Sit down, Gwen. I am not finished the story.'

What more could there possibly be? My shoulders drooped as I squatted on the silk rug and tried to find a way out of the maze of smooth, shiny coloured threads.

'Later that evening, Dr Nag visited again. He was eager to fill me in on the details of removing the membrane. "This lesser common unknown type of caul tissue, which was adhered to the face and head by attachment points, was looped behind the ears, which made the removal process more complex. First, I unlooped it from behind the ears and carefully removed it from her face. It is your daughter's. Put it in a very, very safe place for her. Your sixth child…you will never have to worry about her, but she will have challenges." He fixed his gaze on your face. "This is not an everyday occurrence, Mother. This is very special, auspicious – one in a million. You must keep this veil safely for your sixth child."'

My mother said that she had never understood what the doctor meant and, at the time of my birth, she was only concerned that I was okay. Nurses had fussed around to get a closer look at the caul and insisted that sailors would pay a fortune for such a talisman. When my parents were ready to take me home from the hospital, nurses asked if they could have the caul, but the doctor was firm that my parents keep it.

Mummy pushed the gold-embossed box in my direction.

I recoiled. 'I don't want it, Mummy.'

'Gwen, I know that things are different for you, compared to other children. And I do not know what to do about it, or how to help you.'

I had no idea what things were different for me. I didn't know that I was different from anyone that I knew. I thought that everyone saw and talked to the same people that I did. My mother was firm that that was not the case.

So far, in my young years of life, I didn't think that I had received any luck from this special birth of mine. If I was so lucky, why were my tram fares disappearing into my sister Hannah's pocket on a regular basis, for something other than my fares home from school? My carefully pressed school uniform, socks and polished shoes swiped and used by her? I hadn't got any extra clothes or anything, not even some lipstick to try on like Hannah did when Catherine got a parcel of make-up from her friend in England. There were pictures of the Beatles on their caps and lids. All I got to do was look on while Hannah tried on some Beatles lipstick when Catherine was at work. It wasn't really Hannah's fault; Catherine had been showing them off.

'When will the lucky bits come, Mummy?'

'I don't know, Gwen.'

Mummy massaged her temples and I wondered if she had one of her migraines.

My mother's head pounded often, but that was not surprising. With our father gone for long hours each day, she carried the load of child-rearing. Mummy was never quite sure of his return as it would depend on everything from what had to be published to when a general strike would break out, either in-office or on the streets. Nevertheless, she found the time to remind us that we had British ancestry.

For my mother, along with her love of animals, creativity and religion, her English ancestry took a high place. On her maternal side, she came from a long stock of English. Her great-grandfather, Sir William Fothergill Cooke, was an English inventor, who co-invented with Charles Wheatstone, of Cooke-Wheatstone, the world's first electrical telegraph company, patented in May 1837.

On her paternal side too, there was a long line of English ancestry, with a sprinkle of Portuguese on the line of her great-grandmother, which gave some of us in our family our tanned skin, dark eyes and hair. As a teenager, I proclaimed that I was born in India, therefore Indian – a clear mistake on my part. Mummy was quick in her clarification that her children were Anglo-Indian, not Indian. We were often referred to section 366(2) of India's constitution for verification. All this helped confirm was that it was excellent bait for Mummy that would bring a strong reaction.

Before my departure for India, I had looked at my caul, almost as if I needed something tangible to connect me with my birth land, even though caul births are not specific to India.

Retrieving the gold-embossed cardboard box, six inches in circumference, from its treasured place, I cautiously removed the lid. With trepidation, I peeled back the particular paper that it had been wrapped in since my birth, the amniotic membrane carefully folded within. I touched the silveriness of its rainbow-coloured veins that criss-cross it like a spider's web. It was one of the few times in my entire life that I had looked inside this box closely. Previously, it was a moment usually shared with my mother. Now, I wondered why this membrane wasn't dehydrated? What had enabled it to hold its luminosity and structure? Why hadn't this talisman crumpled and turned to dust? Surely that's what should have happened!

I can't say for sure if it had a bearing on who I am today, or whether it had any bearing on my experiences, but reflecting on the years that have passed, and the doctor's predictions of my fortunate life, I believe it has.

For a visit to my childhood home, I dress in a white cotton, embroidered traditional salwar kameez outfit, a purchase from the previous day. Confident that I no longer stand out as a foreigner, I enter the dining room.

Diana looks at me from head to toe. 'You even want to dress like an Indian now.'

'It will help me blend.'

I wish Diana a good day, and head to the Park Circus tram depot. I don't know which tram will get me to Elliot Road, the location of my early childhood home.

A man in a khaki transport uniform is nearby and willing to assist. 'Number 25, leaving now, ma'am.'

Considering it my luck that the front row seat is vacant, I settle in as the tram snakes out of the depot.

The conductor sidles up to me and indicates with a hand gesture that he wants me to move to the back of the tram, 'Ladies only that way, ma'am.'

'I want to sit here.'

He continues to hold his hand out, ushering me towards the back. Women and girls straighten their head coverings, fidget in their seats. With downcast eyes, they look at me then away.

I don't move.

'Go to back section, back section. Front section for men only.'

My salwar kameez camouflage is broken – a prize peacock being observed by women of all ages. Frustrated, I stomp down the back.

The tram travels at a dreary slow speed, with the bell constantly ringing for something or someone to move out of its way. The streets are brimming with daily life that enthrals and my camera gets to work – snap, snap, snap.

'Ticket, ticket.' The conductor is by my side. 'Ticket, ma'am, four rupees.'

A flimsy green paper ticket not much bigger than a postage stamp is released from the grip of a rubber band and handed to me.

'Please tell me when I get to Elliot Road.'

Under a canopy of cerulean sky, in the dry and dusty compound of my childhood home, I stand bewildered. I recall the twenty-something houses in our locality and outdoor play area as being far more spacious. The fence next door, restraining white geese, chickens and ducks from wandering into other properties, is gone. Iron grilles covering windows and doors are further secured with padlocks. The front yard is desolate, yet the sounds of glass marbles clanging together, tops spinning, and the cries of joy when a seeker located someone in a game of hide and seek, is fresh to my ears. I feel that my soul remained here when my body left.

'Namaste, ma'am. Are you looking for someone?' A woman with dark skin and deep smoky, kohl-lined eyes, swathed in a red and gold sari, greets me. One end of her sari is draped over her head, screening out her entire face, except for her eyes. A toddler hoisted at her hip is wearing nothing but a black thread bangle around a leg – to ward off curses from evil glares. The woman struggles bringing her hands together in prayer position to greet me.

'Namaste.' I return the gesture, and raise a hand toward my family's once home. 'I lived here.'

The woman nods, turns and walks away, as if to give me privacy, or so I think. Minutes later, a swarm of sari-clad women, with heads covered and children in tow, surround me. The children touch me as if to test that I am real. My presence creates no alarm and with a smile I get the head wobble, we-know-you-are-Anglo-Indian. There are no Anglo-Indian families living in this compound, except for my childhood friend, Melvyn. My clothing camouflage, already broken on the tram, now seems totally useless. The only person being fooled is me, but I am comfortable in it. The women's eyes are almost talking, in what I interpret as approval for me to look around. A goat slurping water at the nearby water hydrant, clad in a Nike jacket to keep it warm on this cool winter's day, amuses me. I gesture to it and laugh; they join in. But the interest in me dissipates as quickly as it arrived, or was it so?

Alone, I face my family's once fashionable mosaic veranda floor; it is now pitted concrete. The double-storey building has bricks poking through and there are chips in the rendering. Timber bannisters are faded, starved of polish. Although saddened by the sight, there is joy in being back in a memorable space. I wish I could look inside the house, with its spacious rooms that housed our family of ten, including my paternal Nana. Although that is not possible today, in my mind's eye, Daddy is at the large enamel oven, removing a batch of biscuits that he has baked. It was unforgettable that Daddy found some pleasure in this little exercise, because usually Daddy couldn't boil water, leave alone cook. Servants prepared meals and did all household chores. Then, none of us could prepare a meal, except for our Nana, who enjoyed it. I can almost smell the sweet dumplings that she made on extra special occasions.

I wander to the back of the house, noting that the large tamarind tree that slouched its wide branches on rooftops and balconies is missing. Home to families of swallows, pigeons, crows and a myriad of other creatures, but mostly the cheeky simians that often made their way into homes to help themselves to fruit and shiny objects. I picture Nelson on his way down the tree, following a retrieval mission of his runaway pet squirrel, with bloodied fingers as the creature gnawed on them.

The guava trees, all these years later, still flourish. Once, they had not only provided fruit with a lemon scent and pink flesh, but opportunities to climb and explore. They were also backdrops for camping and many other antics, together with numerous grazes and falls. In the backyard, we often found a trail of discarded snake skins, witnessed the birth of kittens and the hatching of chicken and duck eggs. In the bushes, chrysalises were monitored until butterflies emerged. I remember walking around with a string attached to a wrist and a dragonfly with its tail tied on the other end of it.

Again at the front of the house, I lean back along the bumpy outdoor kitchen wall to soak in the memory, and my fingers brush its exposed bricks. Instantly, I sense that every brick has a story to tell of the first nine years of my life and the memories flow.

The veranda is where Nelson, Hannah, Alison and I sat on Thursday mornings, our regulated day off school. Neighbourhood children joined us in waiting for the monkey keeper, a bag of bones secured in weathered skin. Clad in loose dusty rags, a troupe of monkeys in tow, all held together by ropes of various lengths. The female macaques wore headbands with bows, or magenta tulle frilled skirts, the males in kurta and pyjamas.

Although I kept my distance from them, their weekly visits were welcomed. The keeper sliced bananas with a penknife and, from leathery hands, shared it amongst his charges. A mature male macaque scratched his rear end while the matriarch busily flicked up fur from their young, extracted nits or bugs, and ate them. The procedure was completed with licks to smooth and clean their fur as a final touch-up before their performance, a repertoire of simple jumps and twirls from the young ones.

The adult male cycled on a miniature bicycle to the tune of 'Daisy, Daisy give me your answer do…' The female, clad in an overused greyish-white bridal gown, had a bouquet of flattened artificial roses at the crutch of an elbow. Threading a free hand through the stylish groom's left one, the two were ready for a wedding ceremony that was conducted by the keeper. At its conclusion, the newlyweds made kissing gestures, held hands and encircled the celebrant. In appreciation, spectators dropped a few paisas into a tin plate. In the weeks that followed, they were married again and again.

The monkeys were waved off in time to welcome a lanky seven-foot sloth bear led on a rope; with lips protruded as if ready to kiss. Beside the shaggy brown bear, a barefoot, scantily clad keeper looked small and feeble.

Children hastened to form a circle around the new entertainment and the local Alsatian bared his teeth, puffed the sides of his mouth in a low growl. Unconcerned with the midget animal, the bear rose up on his hind legs that were shorter than his front ones. To the deep rhythm of a tabla, drum, the animal circled, clawing at the air with his sickle shaped claws. Children applauded.

At the end of each performance, the keeper pulled out a bronze bowl from his dusty calico over-the-shoulder bag and invited the children to fill it with paisa. If they obliged, he allowed them to pat the bear. The bear was treated to an apple for his efforts, and the full bowl was emptied into the calico bag. Then the duo was waved off.

The servants' children are running around in circles, chasing and clapping in glee. I am taken with their clean scrubbed faces and dusty legs.

A drumbeat in the distance returns me to the deep repetitive beats when I ran around here with dusty legs. The servants' children were never invited to play games with us or to partake in shows. Perhaps they were never encouraged to play with us either.

Then, the rhythms from tablas often took me to a serene and enchanted space, where I surrendered. I attempt to recall that place, that feeling, but it doesn't return. I ponder, was that a childhood fantasy or the beginning of something more spiritual for me? I cannot be certain and hope my homecoming helps me unravel its meaning.

I am stuck with this thought, when three *hijras*, transvestite eunuchs, approach me. Hairy legs and thick-soled feet hidden under saris, clownish red lipstick outlining their mouths, but entirely missing their lips. I take it all in my stride, and give them a few rupees and they leave. I remember the reactions of previous times when they wandered into our afternoon's events.

Back then, *hijras* only intended to cash in on the already assembled crowd, to beg or perform a dance, play an instrument in exchange for a few coins. Instead, they created a storm of fear. Children squealed and covered their eyes at the sight. Ayahs spat in the dirt in disgust, 'Chi, chi,' in a tone as if they had tasted something offensive then hurried the children indoors. The fear could unnecessarily reach cosmic heights. Anglo-Indians in our locality were more than likely preconditioned that *hijras* carried some form of malevolence, but that was not true. Our community didn't know that *hijras* played important roles in the society of south Asian culture, and we had no reason to fear them.

I pull my shawl tightly around me, hold in the strong memories of childhood – running in the dirt, chasing the geese next door and our strong neighbourly bonds. In the distance, I see an upright sturdy gentleman approaching. Is this déjà vu? The lightweight slacks, cotton shirt, cardigan and sandals resemble my childhood neighbour's father. As the figure draws nearer, the sunlight mapping the lines on his face throws a shadow over his greying brow. At five foot five, we are equal in height, our eyes meet and I see a glint in his.

I hesitate. 'Melvyn?' I say.

'It is nice to see you, Gwen. It has been a very long time, but I would recognise the resemblance of your family features anywhere.'

'It's good to see you, too.'

He even speaks like his father, with the words rolling off his tongue at the speed of a runaway train. Together, in the compound we walk for a while and I kick up dust under my feet.

Melvyn gives a hearty chuckle. 'Forever young.'

His words resonate deep within me.

'When was the water tank removed, Melvyn?' My voice surprises me because it is cracking.

He picks up on the shattering of my words, but skates away from the question. 'Are you tired, Gwen?'

'Perhaps a tad...'

'Do you want a rest? Not necessary to see everything now.'

'Can't believe that water tank incident still gives me the shivers.'

'Let us not talk about that now, it was over forty years ago. Would you like to come to my place, have a rest first, continue down memory lane later?'

We step through double doors and face the dimly lit stairwell to Melvyn's house. The room at the bottom of the stairwell is closed. I pause, half expecting it to open as it always did and for a hunchbacked, wizened woman to appear for a chat.

'Come on. Have you forgotten the way, Gwen?'

'No, it's just... Anyone live in this space now?'

'No one ever lived under there. It is a storage room.'

'Didn't your neighbour Bill's mother live in it?'

Melvyn looks at me as if to say, long flight, eh? 'Bill's mother died long before we were born. Besides, I have never seen an old woman under there.'

'Are you sure? I used to talk to her whenever I came to your place.'

'Of course, I am sure.'

Puzzled with his response, I wonder, is this a reason that my mother disliked me being outside after sunset? Trapped on the spot, I change the subject. 'Do Bill Kerr and his family still live here?'

'They have all gone. He had a restraining order from his wife. He used to beat her to a pulp, you know.' Melvyn takes my hand and leads me upstairs.

I didn't know. To me, that was impossible. They threw parties for their children and Bill always got the *choi*-bags – a bamboo frame shaped into a comic character or an animal. It was covered with papier-mâché and painted or had bright coloured streamers pasted on. They'd fill it with puffed-up rice, plastic jewellery, sweets and trinkets. He would sing 'Happy birthday to you…' while he hung it by a rope from the centre of the ceiling of their party room, which also happened to be their bedroom and lounge room for a family of ten. While the birthday cake was being cut, Bill would blindfold himself and strike the bag with a stick. Children scrambled on the floor amidst puffed-up rice, collecting the goodies that fell from the broken bag. Occasionally, you got a little extra, a bit of grit in your eye or an ant in your hair.

Melvyn's wife, Becky, is at work today. I settle on the lounge and his ayah brings us a tea tray and Nimki biscuits.

Bill a wife basher? My hands tremble as I lift my teacup off the centre table.

'It was wonderful to receive your letter after all these years, Gwen. I never thought I would ever see a member of your family again, once you all vanished overnight – I mean, went to Australia.'

'Honestly, Melvyn, it was a stab in the dark. I didn't know if you still lived here but hoped that somehow the letter would reach you. And, yes, our departure from India had to be a secret affair.'

'Why is that?'

'An ongoing business situation… Something in the kitchen smells nice.'

'You must join me for lunch. I will not take no for an answer. Let me check on cook.'

Melvyn's parents' English-style antique sofa has been refurbished. New floral gabardine cushions propped at either corner, curtains to match. There is a distinct smell of fresh paint. All of this is traditional for Anglo-Indian families who repaint and renew drapery annually, for the joyous season.

Rainbow-coloured crepe paper streamers are strung from the corners of the ceiling, meeting at its centre, flutter in the breeze. On the veranda, trays of fruit covered with muslin are drying on tables. The soft winter's sun settling on them, like butterflies on leaves. From the corner of an eye, I glimpse tinsel glittering on the Christmas tree and feel nostalgic.

4

For my Anglo-Indian family, a trip to the New Market heralded the official start of the Christmas season. The market had been there for almost a century, yet the 'New' in its name remained. Hand-pulled rickshaws carried us to the entrance and delivered memsahib and her brood of four. The rickshaw wallah waited all day for our return. Beggar children covered in a thin film of dust held out grimy hands for a few coins. Chickens in wicker baskets flapped wildly, sending small downy feathers floating into the street.

Inside the market, the majority of vendors, without individual shops, displayed their wares from concrete platforms that were raised a metre above ground. Legs crossed on gunnysacks, they called to passersby, boasting a guarantee of the best quality, best price and the only one of its type available in the entire bustling market today.

The first purchase of the day for memsahib was curtain fabric. Bolts of fabric, in cotton, polyester or a mixture of both, floral, plain, plaid were reeled off, layer upon layer, as if they were puff pastry, for Mummy's pleasure. Nothing appealed. Memsahib and her entourage moved on to the next shop, where the entire process was repeated. Two or three hours and many displays of fabric later, Mummy returned to the first shop that she had visited to make a selection.

Now that memsahib had the upper hand knowing all the market prices for the day, she made an offer.

The vendor scoffed at the suggestion, throwing his hands in the air with disgust. 'You are killing me, memsahib. This is the best price, please.' He rocked his head as if it were a seesaw as he rolled up the bolts of fabric.

Mummy walked away.

The vendor, obviously keen for a sale, chased Mummy from shop to shop. 'Memsahib, I am giving you the best price, please. Memsahib, buy something please.'

Mummy was the vendor's first customer of the day and it was the second time that morning that she had walked out of his shop. Although he had had other customers since her first visit, he was unwilling to give up. As superstition had it, if the first customer of the day did not buy something, there would be no or very poor sales for the day.

During purchases of unsalted butter, blanched almonds and glacé cherries, the vendor secured a sale of curtain fabric. The entire entourage returned to the fabric shop, where the merchant measured fabric under Mummy's watchful eye, to ensure that the merchant didn't include the ink stamp that was at the beginning of each fabric roll. The purchase wrapped in newspaper required a coolie being hired to carry the load. He followed us around for the rest of the day, stacking all future purchases in a fine balance on his head.

By the time we had bought shoes and socks, Mummy was tired from her morning haggling with vendors and wanted a break. We all piled into the nearest teahouse. While having her tea, Mummy kept a close eye on the coolie. He of course tried to remain out of sight. He did not want to be considered disrespectful, which he would be if she were to see him smoking a *bidi*. Alarmed that she could not see him, she brought the tea session to a halt.

There, with metres of crêpe de Chine, cotton and taffeta for the girls, twill or wool for Daddy and Nelson, undergarments and shoes, our shopping day ended.

Back home, Mummy got one of her usual Christmas shopping headaches, took two Aspros and went to bed.

Without prompting, children prepared Christmas cake ingredients. Orange fruit peel, pawpaw, glacé cherries, white pumpkin and nuts were chopped, sliced, diced and spread on trays, covered with muslin and left in the sunshine to dry for a couple of weeks. In the process, the eager helpers sampled all the ingredients.

The next morning, 'Ma, I think that thief of a shopkeeper's scales are out. There should be more ingredients than this,' Mummy said to Nana, our paternal grandmother.

From the tone of Mummy's voice, we children knew it was best to look busy and stay out of the conversation. We straightened coverings on trays and moved them around, all in an effort to look innocent and helpful.

'Next year I'm going to keep a closer watch on that thief and his scales,' Mummy harped, while she checked that there was sufficient brandy and port wine to soak the dried fruit and peel.

Each year, the quantities were increased, as were arguments with vendors about faulty scales, and although they each put a little extra in to appease Mummy, there was always a considerable shortage after her helpful elves had given a hand.

Indian mynah birds are sitting on Melvyn's balcony squabbling. Each bird then takes a place on the railing, almost as if by instruction. Watching this took me back to Christmas cake baking day, when children squabbled over the best place to sit, and Mummy tried to organise us.

On the day before the bakers arrived, the drawing room was cleared of furniture and the floor covered in plastic-backed, white cotton sheeting. A dozen or so twelve-inch round baking tins and a tester size six-inch one was lined with greaseproof paper. Flour, butter, eggs, vanilla, bottled secret spices and prepared fruit were arranged in aluminium containers in front of the mixing bowls.

Adults sat on chairs behind the ingredients, bowls and tins; children sat on the floor in a row, below the adults.

The local baker and his offsider arrived around mid-morning, dressed in white baker's beret, bibbed apron and neckerchief. They brought their own mixing spoons, spatulas, and two stainless steel bowls, which were large enough to bath a baby.

Dozens of egg whites were whisked, butter creamed, flour folded. Prepared fruit stirred in, under the instruction and watchful eye of the memsahib with her 'special' unique Christmas cake recipe – the pride of every Anglo-Indian home, with no other household sharing the exact same recipe. The hand or the eye of the baker judged all measurements.

At intervals, memsahib interrupted the procedure. 'A little more fruit please, and an extra dash of spice.'

'Yes, memsahib.' He added more until…

'That will be sufficient.'

The bakers mixed and stirred until Mummy was satisfied, then filled cake tins.

'You need to make a Madeira cake for sahib. He doesn't like fruit-cake.'

A fresh bowl and ingredients were made available.

Children were allowed the bowls and wooden spoons to scrape out any remnants of mixture to sample right away. Strips of white grease-proof paper, with the family name on it, were placed on the top of each uncooked cake. The bakers loaded them onto a large wooden block, covered them and took them by bullock cart to their bakery ovens.

While waiting for the cakes to be returned that same night, all available family members were recruited for the time-consuming and painstaking *kalkals* (always referred to in the plural). Balls, the size of marbles, made from flour, eggs, milk and soft butter, were spread along the backs of forks. After a firm press down to imprint the fork's pattern on to the dough, it resembled a shell shape. Hundreds of shells later, they were deep fried in batches, rested, then dipped into hot liquid sugar. When cooled they had a white frosty coating. They were stored in airtight tins for the Christmas season.

Following dinner, the baked cakes were returned. Mummy checked for the correct family name. The tasting cake was sliced and shared with family. Once approved, the baker was paid and dismissed.

Melvyn returns to the room, catches me in a daydream. 'A penny for your thoughts.'

'I was reminiscing about my Christmases in India, Melvyn.'

Melvyn gives me a warm smile and walks with a glass in hand to a nearby sideboard. He opens a cabinet door as if he is going to pour a drink. Instead, he pulls out a shoebox. Its contents, piles of black and white photos from our childhood and photos of my family, surprise me.

'I never knew you had these photos, Melvyn. Who took them?'

'My mother did and after she expired, I decided to keep them because I knew your family.'

The first photo is of the neighbourhood children – barefoot, setting up a game of seven tiles. They were not real tiles, but instead flat stones that could be stacked on top of each other, only to be bowled over within minutes. Two teams took turns in knocking players in the opposite team out by hitting them with a ball below the knees when they tried to restack the fallen tiles. Melvyn and I both rub below our knees as if we feel the sting of being struck.

From the pile, Melvyn pulls a picture of my father, with oldest sister Patricia on her wedding day. She is on Daddy's arm, her face hidden behind a fine tulle veil, her head bowed, as if she is looking down for her flower girls – Hannah, Alison and me – in organza dresses, with colours from the rainbow, and matching floral headbands. Each one of us clutching a silver cane basket filled with rose petals. Daddy is wearing a dark tailored suit, white shirt, black cummerbund and shiny black shoes. He looks the very picture of his pukka, perfect English upbringing.

Daddy's fair skin and sophisticated nose ruled him out to pass for Indian. Yet he managed to master the Indian art of balling up rice and lentils with three fingers, or should I say, two and two-third fingers, one third having been crushed in an industrial machine. He popped the ball into his mouth, as if he were a thoroughbred. Unlike Mummy, who never failed to let us know we had British ancestry and ensured we never went down the Indian path, Daddy had talked of the *Bhagavad Gita*, an extract from the *Mahabaratha*, and the *Ramayan*a, India's two epics.

He also read, commented on and recited lines from the poetry of Rabindranath Tagore.

As a young child, my father had personal experience with one of India's medicinal practices, Unani, a form of alternative medicine, based on the belief that the human body contains four humours – blood, phlegm, yellow and black bile. The imbalance of these was the cause of disease. At age three, when Daddy was admitted to hospital with an abscess in his stomach and all other forms of traditional medicine had failed, an Indian doctor had recommended this form of healing. Herbert, his father, gave permission. Later in life, although Daddy was unable to explain the treatment or even understand how it restored him to good health, he remained open to other forms of medicine.

During his business life, while traversing the country, he expanded his knowledge of India's many diverse cultures, religions and comportments.

Anglo-Indians had attempted to perfect other Indian arts too. They took Indian words and changed them into a lingo of their own – *blithy* (British), bungalow (house), dacoit (criminal), *almira* (wardrobe), cot (bed), veranda (porch), to name a few. Also, Indian dishes were concocted to make it a style of their own – jhalfrazee, meatball curry, yellow rice and *kalkals*. Indian words that couldn't be pronounced properly or sounded different to the Anglo-Indian ear, were changed – dhal became doll.

Around Independence in 1947, it was commonplace for Anglo-Indians to deny India as their birthplace in order to preserve their British 'roots', as if being Indian would somehow tarnish them – Merle Oberon being one of many famous Anglo-Indians who disclaimed their origin.

My father, Samuel, was born during World War I in Madras, India. His great-grandfather, Benjamin, was born 1817, in Bentley, Yorkshire. At the age of twenty-six, Benjamin arrived in India with the British Army as a bombardier for the 2nd Bombay Artillery. Two years later, he married English-born Mary Halpin. Their son, also a Benjamin, and his second wife, Jane Davis, English too, gave birth to Herbert – my paternal grandfather. In 1911, Herbert chose Hannah, the daughter of a

Scottish father and French mother, to be his bride. My father was born five years following their marriage and his sister, Myrtle, a decade later.

Herbert was employed on the Indian Railways, Madras. Anglo-Indians were the backbone of and dominated the Indian Railway network before and immediately after Indian Independence. In his leisure, Herbert was a professional musician. The serving Governor of Madras, Lord Willingdon, had an exclusive governor's band. He invited Herbert to join as a trombone player. In accepting the position, Herbert and my grandmother were given quarters and resided in Government House, Madras.

The governor's wife, Lady Willingdon, forged a lasting friendship with my grandmother and appointed herself surrogate godmother to my father, because, she claimed, 'She saw a child with potential.'

Lady Willingdon took it upon herself to organise for Samuel, at age three, to attend a private preschool outside Madras – exclusive to the children of the governor's staff, as a boarder, away from his parents. My grandmother, outraged with the decision to send her young son so far away from her, took him out of the school. Lady Willingdon was furious and forbade the school to allow his parents to take him out, even on weekends and holidays.

While Samuel was attending preschool, the Prince of Wales, who would later become King Edward VIII, visited Madras. Lady Willingdon introduced him to Samuel. The prince gave the small child a paper boat. Samuel launched his boat straight away and, to his disappointment, it collapsed in the water. However, he claimed the prince's visit was etched into his memory. On completing preschool, Samuel's education continued under the guidance of the governor's wife at a school in a nearby valley, bounded by forests, orchards and potato fields. Happy with his surroundings and school life, he excelled. An unrivalled athlete, he was nominated to represent his school in boxing, hockey and cricket.

At seventeen, Samuel completed school and returned to Madras. His academic records assisted in his being offered an engineering apprenticeship with *The Mail*, a Madras newspaper. He gained the highest qualifications in electrical and mechanical engineering. At that time, he also gave service to the Madras Contingent (Auxiliary Force, India) AF (I) from 1934 to 1938.

In 1941, the year of his marriage, he accepted the position of deputy superintendent and engineer-in-charge of the *Indian Express* newspaper. A few years later, he left Madras for Calcutta, to join *The Statesman*. He gained credentials in the printing and publishing industry and eventually achieved the highest position within the company as printer and publisher for India's largest and most widely read newspaper at that time, a position that held him responsible for everything that was published in the paper, whether he was at his desk or not. Government election times proved to be a difficult time for Daddy and the entire family. Political publications were challenged for misrepresenting or failing to represent certain political parties sufficiently, and on occasions retaliation could be made against Daddy or his family.

During the company's industrial disputes, Daddy acted as mediator with disgruntled employees. His work often took him interstate, especially to the national capital, Delhi. It was seldom that he forgot to bring treats for the children, even if he only went for the day.

Daddy took an active role in the Anglo-Indian movement along with other prominent Anglo-Indians, representing his community in various capacities. Following Indian Independence, Daddy as a State Council member (1945–1971), made representations in the all-India delegations which formulated the rules that governed the movement to establish a position for Anglo-Indians in the Indian Constitution.

My father reported on many major national and global events. He often told of the personal shock that he felt in January 1948, when Mahatma Gandhi was assassinated, and his responsibility in reporting the devastating incident that shook India. Daddy had met the Mahatma as a young man and then again only days before this tragedy shook India.

Discussions for an independent India concluded with a British government-commissioned report which divided the country into India and Pakistan. Inhabitants of India were not only attached to their religious distinctiveness but also their land. And although Pakistan, at Indian Independence, was created as a homeland for Muslims, not all Muslims supported the change. Many remained in India, creating the largest minority group in the country.

This led to considerable violence up to and following independence. Riots and skirmishes created mass casualties. Hundreds of thousands of people were evicted from their homes. Women, targeted as symbols of community, were raped and murdered. Mahatma Gandhi, a Hindu, leader of the Indian non-violent independence movement, father of the Indian nation and guiding light, sought peace and tolerance. The Mahatma practised Satyagraha non-violence and undertook a fast to death, an action he often engaged in to protest. On this occasion, it was to shame those who partook in and provoked violence. World leaders and the founder of the newly created Pakistan, Mohammed Ali Jinnah, commended him for his concerns about amity.

But some Hindu fanatics detested the Mahatma's call for peace, complaining that it prevented Hindus from protecting themselves against attacks, and called for his death. A Hindu fanatic set off a bomb near the Mahatma but he was unscathed. Ten days later, weakened by his fast, the Mahatma was walking across the lawn of Birla House, New Delhi, where he had been staying. About five hundred people were waiting for him to lead them in a prayer meeting. A Hindu fanatic concealed in the Mahatma's approving crowd broke free and shot him point blank in the stomach and chest.

'Where else in India do you plan to travel during this trip, Gwen?' said Melvyn.

'I'm the family's self-appointed historian, so a trip to my parents' and grandparents' places of birth and death is on the itinerary. In my father's memory, I am keen to walk in his footsteps in Delhi. Then the Taj Mahal of course. Definitely a visit to Varanasi. I will return to Kolkata before I head back home to Sydney.'

Melvyn's brow creases, 'You must have a keen interest in yoga to visit Varanasi.'

'Well, yes. Sorry, have I failed to tell you about that interest of mine?'

'How did it come about?'

'I have a natural aptitude for the Indian modalities of yoga, meditation, Ayurveda.'

'But Anglo-Indians don't follow these traditions.'

'That may be, but I began doing yoga very soon after going to Australia, delved into other Indian techniques and continue with them to date. My first teacher was a non-Indian woman, Roma Blair, who took yoga to Australia, and in 1967 set up the International Yoga Teachers' Association, not long before we arrived in Australia. At that time, I didn't know that later on in life, I would join the organisation and go on to lecture for them. I not only learned, but now also teach yoga.'

With his thumb and index finger, Melvyn traces from his lower jawbone to his chin, drums his fingers on it and sharply turns away. 'Let me check in with cook.'

It saddens me that Melvyn and Diana are so shocked at me doing yoga, something that is a big and important part of my life and had originated in India.

Melvyn returns to the room. 'Lunch is ready.' He leads the way to the table.

The cook looks unstable juggling a tray with steam escaping from a speciality rice dish – biryani. Also, curries of chicken, fish and vegetables, garnished with sliced lemon and coriander leaves. Baskets of naan bread, platters of tandoori paneer soon follow. His ayah brings a jug of water to the table and it must remind Melvyn.

'How did you end up in the water tank, that fretful monsoon day?'

'Unfortunate situation,' I skate over the question. 'Thank you, this lunch looks and smells delicious. Are you expecting dozens of guests?' I laugh.

'Just us.'

'I must say, Melvyn, hospitality in India is second to none.'

Lunch is a long slow procedure, with many favourite dishes as well as discussion, ranging from family happenings over the years to what Australians love.

I chuckle. Australians had a favourite jingle for that when we first arrived in Australia, but I stop short of bellowing it. 'Sport, cars, gambling, beaches, drinking together, and barbecues. They are a laid-back people.'

Melvyn nods in acknowledgement.

I have over-indulged with food and feel the need to walk. Melvyn has picked up on my mood. 'Ready to continue down memory lane?'

5

The wire gate bumps and scrapes along the dirt as Melvyn forces it open. We are at the spot where the water tank once stood. The apprehension from years past on that monsoon day in a cool and darkened tank surface once more. I look down at my fingers expecting them to be shrivelled, but of course they are not. I experience the hopelessness of that day when trapped in the tank and tremble inside, not realising that it has externalised.

'Are you all right?' asks Melvyn with knitted brows.

'Yes, I'm fine.' I force a smile.

'You don't look it.'

'I merely experienced a moment of terror reliving that afternoon when Hannah was to join me in play in the tank. We had a precision plan carved out for the visit. Our mother disapproved of us playing in there at monsoon time, so we had to make sure she didn't find out. In fact, our mother was not happy with us being in there at any time.

'I had clambered into the grey metal tank by gripping its rim and sliding down ahead of Hannah's arrival. Water lapped at my toes. 'Hello, hello, hello,' I called. I wanted to hear the echo of my voice in the tank, spinning round me. With each "hello", I jumped higher. When I stood still, tiny tadpoles that we had put in there, swam up to my feet, nibbled at them. I scooped water into a jam jar and with a net, I caught some slimy creatures that wriggled and tipped them into the jar – watched them thrash their tails against the glass.'

'I never knew you played in the tank.'

'It was mostly Nelson, Hannah and I. Especially in the summer months when the tank was bone dry. My godfather had gifted me a cooking set and we often took it into the tank. We lit the miniature stove's cotton wick that trailed into a canister filled with kerosene. Once the flame blazed, we steamed rice and peas. On rare occasions, we invited other children to drop in and share our feast. One day, Lorraine visited us in there. Do you remember her?'

'Her family's property has now been converted into a church. She was crazy about lizards, wasn't she?'

'Always had a pocketful of them. On one particular visit, when she tried climbing out of the tank, she missed her footing on the rope ladder and swung with one arm, as if she were a monkey. Tiny lizards scrambled over her arms and head. We laughed so hard at the sight. But that monsoon day when I was trapped in the tank, there was no rope.' I put my hand on my stomach, smoothed it over in the hope that the topsy-turvy feeling that had begun would subside.

Melvyn raises his eyebrows and I wonder if once again he detects the terror of that day in my eyes.

'When I looked through the gaping hole at the entrance to the tank, all I saw was a circle of grey sky. I heard a clap of thunder, and tried to jump high in an effort to grasp the rim and pull myself up. But at seven years old, I wasn't tall enough to reach the top. With each jump, water splashed out of the jar. Tadpoles plunged to the bottom of the tank. I scooped more water into the jar, gave it a shake and watched the remaining tadpoles ride the waves, envious that they could swim. Poor tadpoles, did they feel trapped too, with only a circular opening above them – too far for them to reach? I tipped them out of the jar, so that they could be free. Again, I looked through the tank's entrance and saw swollen rain clouds gathering, I was terrified. "Hannah, where are you? Where are you?" I called, but she never came. In school, Sister Marie Claire had told us, "When you are troubled, sing. It will make you feel better." "Row, row, row your boat…" I sang, hopeful that Hannah would arrive like she had promised.'

'That must have been terrifying?'

'It was, and rowing wasn't working for me, so I tried another of Sister Marie Claire's songs. "Kookaburra sits in the old gum tree…" I had never seen a kookaburra. I knew that kookaburras laughed, but I was in no mood to laugh anyway. Why had Irish nuns in a school in India taught us a song about a kookaburra? I didn't know. It wasn't as if it was likely we'd see one in Calcutta or maybe that's why they… Anyway, none of that was helping me to get out of the tank. Then I heard the first clap of thunder. The monsoon rain was on its way.

'I had to get out. I turned the jam jar upside down, balanced on it with my left foot. Still not able to reach the rim, I stretched a little higher, and at that precise moment, there was a smothered sound underfoot, followed by sharp pain and I sank a little further down. I knew that the jar had shattered. I changed feet, so as to hold up the hurt one and investigate the pain, but on setting down my unhurt foot, I felt a stab of pain, something warm ooze out from it and it burned. Tears like the monsoon rain flowed. I stumbled around on the outside edges of my feet. The aching, gritty feel beneath my feet made me jump around.'

Melvyn's smile disappears and he shakes his head. 'Did it rain when you were in there?'

'It bucketed down. Rain pelted my head. The inside of the tank grew darker and bleak. I felt abandoned. I realised singing would not be of any use. Besides, I couldn't remember the words even if I wanted to. I cried aloud for help. No one came. I hadn't thought about the water much, until I realised that it was up to my knees. I looked up to the entrance hole and bawled. Rain ran into my mouth and nose, made me gag. My clothes were saturated, my fingers crinkled.

'I knew that the thunder was drowning out my sobs. No one would find me – soon water would swallow me and I'd be gone forever. I needed to be brave and find a way out, but each clap of thunder made me shiver and a plan would not come. I sobbed and called out for an endless time, when I heard, "Gwen, Gw-en."'

'Thank goodness. I bet that cheered you up.'

'At first, I ignored the call, because I thought it was my imagination, but decided to call back. Nothing. I was terrified and I bellowed. My throat hurt, my feet hurt – I began to think no one cared. Water swished and swirled all around me. Exhausted but hopeful that prayer would save me, I began a litany, "Holy Mother, save me, save me…save me…me."

'Then I thought I heard Nelson, but convinced myself that it was my imagination again, I continued with the litany, "Holy Mother…" My holy tears mingled in the water, that rose past my knees. Soon it would engulf me. The time had come to make a confession, to ask, "Please God, forgive me for all my sins – I don't know what they are right now. If disobeying my mother and jumping into the tank is a sin, forgive me. Actually, please forgive me for whatever you think that I have done wrong."

'A faint sound of activity played in my ears, in my mind. Only Hannah knew I was in here and she had forgotten. No one would think to look in the tank.'

'Your mother would have had an entire army out looking for you,' said Melvyn.

'I'm sure she would have, but in my fear, I hadn't thought that anyone would find me, until an outline of a head appeared at the tank's entrance, and a familiar voice echoed, "Gwen, are you in there?"

'I called back to Nelson in my best-effort loud voice, above the clashes of thunder, but felt certain that the rain had washed my voice away. Then I heard Nelson tell me to grab his hand. I reached my hand as high as I could. I couldn't see anything, with rain pouring into my eyes. "I'll be back," he said. And Nelson was gone.

'Once again, tears were my companion. After what felt like an eternity but was probably a couple of minutes, a rope dangled in front of me. I grabbed its rough bristle with both hands. "Gwen, can you pull yourself up?" I heard. "No." "I'll have to pull you up then. Grab the rope, wrap it around yourself, hold it tight."'

Melvyn's jaw drops, his fingers pressed against his chin and his eyes opened wide.

'I wrapped and gripped. Nelson tugged and pulled. I was scraped up and over the rim. Nelson helped me jump down into the flood below. He held my hand as we waded home.'

'Your poor mother must have been relieved to see you.'

I recalled my mother's sorrowful eyes brighten when Nelson got me home. 'My mother never liked me out of her sight for too long, so yes, I guess she would have been. She gave Nelson a pat on the head and a towel, then swathed me in a blanket and wrapped a towel around my hair. Nana wrapped her arms around Nelson and gave me the look, for all the worry that I had caused, I supposed. Especially because I would have put him in danger too and he was her favourite. Later that evening, I could smell Nana's sweet dumplings cooking. I wasn't offered any.

'In the days that followed, I had glass removed from my feet, which was painful, but my family brought me gifts of books, pencils, and sweets in abundance. *Pish-pash,* our favourite Anglo-Indian dish of rice with boneless chicken and a few spices, simmered over a slow fire, a cure-all recipe, together with clear chicken broth for invalids were my meals for the following week. Hannah was regretful that she forgot our meeting and promised that she would remember next time. For me, there would never be a next time.

'It was a dreadful feeling being stuck in the tank, unsure if anyone was coming to save me, Melvyn. I might have drowned,' I said in a somewhat dramatic tone.

'But your brother did find you, Gwen, and here you are safe and sound. We still dread the monsoonal downpours, and scurry to stay dry.'

The endless monsoon days played out in my head – the continuous pat-pat-patter of green-tinged rain falling from swollen, dark clouds, creating inland seas, engulfing whole neighbourhoods and washing away entire sections of alleyways and streets.

Beggars in street dwellings made from cardboard boxes or plastic tarpaulins gathered their belongings and sought shelter under shop awnings, stairwells or anywhere that was higher ground. Traffic got bogged and hand-pulled rickshaws, the one mode of transport to get you from place to place other than on foot, were in high demand. Rickshaw wallahs struggled through deluged streets. Occasionally a wheel got caught in a pothole. Then the entire rickshaw sloped to one side, launching its passengers into panic.

Schoolchildren were sent home at random times, wading in knee- or waist-deep water. At other times, there were whole or multiple days off school. On those occasions, before he left for work, Daddy set us copious amounts of spelling, grammar, books to read and stories to write, all of which had to be completed by his return. In between, Mummy filled in the time with the rosary or a litany.

Still, we found time to make paper boats to float down the streets. With extra time to spare, we tortured each other, which did not amuse Mummy. At night when Daddy returned, Mummy lined us up and presented her complaints. Often, our punishment was more spelling. Visitors did not come over during the monsoons and we rarely saw our neighbours during the long, wet days, except while outdoors – boating!

Indoors, Hannah was inexhaustible with amusements and ways in which to make money. In no time at all, she could create a shop with mini sandwiches, diced fruit and drinks for sale. All of which were made from home supplies, but the takings were exclusively hers. Also, she ran raffles for items that we owned or something that she had acquired through some unknown source. And of course, she was always the lucky winner.

At the end of the monsoons, agile rickshaw wallahs got a reprieve from dodging potholes. Angry passengers, being delivered to their homes, poked the rickshaw wallahs with umbrellas and haggled down the price of a fare. The sun dried the dampness. Paper boats that once floated through the compounds and streets were heaped up in gutters and passageways. Flattened. Street vendors returned, and the aroma of cumin and coriander once more filled the air. Corn, held on wooden sticks, snapped and crackled on open flames. When sold, they were seasoned with butter and pepper or lemon juice.

People stayed outdoors late into the evenings, exuberant with a new lease of life. Games resumed – marbles, and tops with latis firmly wound around. The thin rope, released with speed, made the tops spin faster. When that was an insufficient challenge, another top was discharged on to the current one, splitting it in half and rendering it useless altogether.

'No big changes in this compound, other than removing the water tank and the tamarind tree, on account of the monkeys becoming a nuisance, forcing windows open and taking food, jewellery and whatever else they fancied from nearby homes,' said Melvyn.

'What did they do with the monkeys?'

'They were taken to the city outskirts.'

'I am sure your family related the story to you of the grieving matriarch that took a human baby from its crib, as a substitute for her lost one,' said Melvyn.

'I was the baby next door to them at the time, so glad it wasn't me.'

The Larkin family lived nearest to the tree. The monkeys, with ease of access to their place, helped themselves to their fruit bowl for their daily supply of bananas.

It was in the early hours of one morning. Mrs Larkin was enjoying a cup of tea on her back veranda, which stretched the whole length of their bedrooms. From there, she would hear Lexi, her two-month-old baby wake.

Sitting on a canvas chair soaking in the fresh air and tranquillity of the morning, she heard the muezzin call faithful to the mosque for Fajr, first prayer of the day. Although Mrs Larkin claimed that she didn't believe in anything, when she heard the haunting sound of prayer that morning, she claimed it had touched her in some way.

As the blue light of dawn broke the darkness, Mrs Larkin's attention turned to the giant tamarind tree's large supple branches. Its shady foliage spreading over her roof and drooping over the upstairs railing. She was grateful for the shade it provided on hot summers days. The sun's first rays trickled through the leaves, settling on her face. The tree's inhabitants, simians, began their morning ritual, chattering and swinging from branch to branch. Mrs Larkin noticed a matriarch on her own and wondered what had happened to the little fur ball she had seen her lovingly groom days earlier.

Mrs Larkin readied the breakfast table and hoped that the smell of bacon cooking would awaken Mr Larkin. Before long, the two sat to eat.

Lexi wailed and Mrs Larkin attended her. 'Good morning, my precious Plum Pudding. Did you have a big sleep? Yes, you did, yes, you did...' she cooed and flung open the door to the veranda. 'We like to see that big tree, don't we?'

Out on the veranda, while feeding her newborn a bottle of milk, Mrs Larkin caught sight of the matriarch once again. She then wondered about all the pandemonium in the tree a few days earlier. Her heart melted when she suspected the unfortunate fate of the fur ball. She caressed her baby close to her chest. When the bottle was empty, Mrs Larkin wrapped Lexi tightly in a white muslin shawl and rocked her. Once asleep, she took Lexi indoors, laid her in the cradle, planted a kiss on the soft curl at the crown of her head and tiptoed out of the room.

Mrs Larkin prepared Lexi's next feed and popped it into the icebox on the veranda. 'I'm off to see Gwen, the latest addition in the family next door. I won't be long and you shouldn't hear a peep out of Lexi,' she said to Mr Larkin. Marriage had not changed the way Mrs Larkin addressed her husband, who had his head buried in the morning paper.

'I cannot stay long. Ayah didn't arrive this morning,' she had told my mother.

Smiles and compliments were exchanged. Cups of tea accompanied cucumber sandwiches, cheese straws, mince patties and cakes from the famous Swiss teahouse, Flurys, which caused the visit to last longer than planned.

On her return she called out, 'I'm home, Mr Larkin.'

He was still mulling over the newspaper.

'How has our little Plum Pudding been?'

'Not a stir.'

'Such a lovely baby she is, Mr Larkin.'

A few minutes passed before she poked her head into Lexi's room. 'Where is my lovely Plum Pudding?' she yelled.

Mr Larkin threw the paper aside and together they ran from room to room, as if by some mysterious chance Lexi would be in one of them. Mrs Larkin wept and called for her Plum Pudding over and over.

They ran downstairs and into the compound, where they ran around in circles for a while. Their hysteria drew a group of servants to them. They tried to explain that their baby was missing but soon realised that the servants did not understand what they said. Mr Larkin raced to the backyard. Mrs Larkin kept crying and calling, 'Plum Pudding', until exhausted she fell to the ground. Servants helped her to her feet and even though she cried out that Plum Pudding had gone missing, they did not seem particularly concerned.

'Memsahib,' said one of the servants, 'It is not yet Christmas time, you don't have plum puddings now for anyone to take.'

With Mr Larkin now at her side, the two realised the confusion that she had created about Plum Pudding. They attempted to explain that their baby had gone missing out of her crib. Together they yelled in broken Hindi/English, *'Baccha, baccha*, gone, *sona.'*

Neighbours had come out to see what the commotion was about. Mrs Larkin, a mass of nerves, jittered, wiping away tears from eyes that took on a faraway vacant look. They helped clear up the confusion and it became clear to all that Mrs Larkin's baby, Lexi, had gone missing.

Mr Larkin assembled a search party under the tamarind tree. Speculation took place as to the baby's whereabouts. Children in these neighbourhoods never went missing. Ever. Mr Larkin was certain that no one had entered their home while Mrs Larkin was absent. At last, a conclusion was reached that Lexi could only have been taken through the back door, but that was impossible. They would have to scale down a floor with a baby in tow and then over the brick wall at the rear of the residences.

'We have to call the police,' said Mr Larkin.

'Sahib, don't call police, they do nothing. We can find and handle the thieves much quicker than police, in our way. Yes,' said the servant group all together.

Everyone agreed that calling the police would be a waste of time. The search party led by Mr Larkin was broken into small groups – that way they could quickly cover more area. Each unit was given instructions and assigned a range. The newly formed groups were on their way when the unmistakable cry of a young baby hollered from above. Everyone looked up to the high branches. They did not need to second-guess a muslin shawl being rocked by the matriarch whose infant was missing.

Mrs Larkin howled and shook her fist at the beast, until she recognised a milk bottle as the one she had placed in the icebox earlier that morning being directed toward the shawl and the cry ceased.

Mother-to-mother she reasoned, 'Look, I love my baby, I know you want her too, but she's mine. Please bring her back. I am not sure what happened to your baby and I am so sorry for your loss but please give my baby back, back…' Her legs buckled and she crashed once more to the dirt.

The throng of people shook fists at the matriarch and yelled.

'Be quiet,' Mr Larkin cautioned them, 'Don't panic the animal.'

Hostage to a monkey, the search party was at a standstill. The couple of minutes in silence had given time to gather thoughts and qualify each of them with instant degrees in monkey psychology. They foraged and gathered shiny objects and baskets laden with bananas. The monkey community chattered amongst themselves. Eager, they displayed teeth now that food and treasure were available in readiness. The search party waited in anticipation and tried to be as quiet as possible.

A withered holy man, with white hair down to his waist and a long and thinning beard, hobbled his way through the crowd on a timeworn walking stick. 'Leave monkey be, leave monkey be.' He held his stick up high and ordered the crowd away from the tree, 'The monkey is a symbol of Hanuman, one of the most popular idols in the Hindu pantheon.'

'I'll crack your skull open with that walking stick if you don't put it down.' Mrs Larkin shouted.

It was obvious that he didn't understand what she said. He raised a triangular saffron flag, chanting, *'Najrangbali Ki Jai,* victory to thy thunderbolt strength.' His chant reverberated and he held his frail hand out to Mrs Larkin on the ground.

She refused it. Her husband helped steady her to her feet and she clung to Mr Larkin's arm. Together, they stood helplessly glaring up at the simian with their baby. They both knew that if they panicked the simian, any chance of Lexi's safe return was in jeopardy.

In her moments of terror, although distraught, Mrs Larkin noticed that the holy man's chant dissipated her anger. For a brief moment, she felt calm, a sense of control over mind and body prevailed. At brief spells, she caught some of his words about the greatness of the Monkey god but thought it ridiculous that she even entertained that thought. It was mumbo-jumbo stuff to her. 'Be quiet,' she cried.

A group of people sat around the holy man and, as he told the legend of this mythical character, they watched him in awe. It irritated Mrs Larkin that the crowd forgot about the baby and swayed with his every movement, and when he leaped around as if in flight, they did too.

'Go away!' She stomped at him.

He pointed his walking stick skyward. The eyes of his followers widened, and they now appeared to be able to see first-hand the legend of which he spoke.

Then he prayed, 'Oh, Great one who has aided Lord Rama in his expedition against evil force, Avatar of Lord Shiva; give us your strength, your abilities to face this ordeal and conquer the obstructions that hold us back.' He stopped, faced the crowd and continued, 'Fellow men, God has found it necessary with his action to teach us an important lesson, that there is an unlimited power unused within each one of us.

Greatness rests in the merger with the Lord. This is the symbol of Hanuman, the great simian monkey god.'

A follower translated his prayer.

At the time, Mrs Larkin did not care or even know that he was drawing reference to two of the most important ancient epics of India: the *Ramayana* and the *Mahabharata*. Mr Larkin stayed close to his wife. The two twitched with anger and alarm, eyes fixed at activities high in the tree.

Surrounded by his followers' chants of what Mrs Larkin considered to be prayers, she too now felt the urge to pray, but didn't know the words. The holy man waved the saffron flag again. She had lost the desire to even complain at his intrusion. Catholic women prayed the rosary.

Sensitive to Lexi's whimpers from the tree, Mrs Larkin watched every movement. The matriarch cradled the muslin shawl bundle, rocked it with tenderness and puckered her lips at a dark mop that poked out at the top. Mrs Larkin muffled her cry when a lactating female, distinguishable by protruding nipples, approached the matriarch. The muslin bundle was bestowed with precision. Mrs Larkin held her breath but was dumbstruck by the affection shown.

With eyes fixated, Mrs Larkin gasped as Lexi's latest caregiver placed the bundle under an arm and swung up a few branches. Simultaneously, Plum Pudding released a loud cry. Alarmed, the newfound guardian lost her grip on the shawl and Lexi plummeted.

Mrs Larkin screamed, her ribs expanded with her heaving chest, and she clutched at her hair, pulling at clumps until it stood on edge, as if she had received an electric shock. 'My baby, baby…' she bellowed. Her body statue-like, her face concealed in terror.

The matriarch reached out an arm to the hysterical baby, snatched her up. The muslin shawl was released and baby legs dangled. With a yank, the matriarch pulled the bundle close to her body, rocked it in frenzy. Lexis's cries amplified, which seemed to agitate the matriarch further and she swung from branch to branch, an object coming loose from the matriarch's clutches. The crowd roared as an accompaniment to the hurtling article and mattresses were rushed under it for a soft fall, but it skimmed the edge of a mattress and bounced off. Glass splintered on the ground.

Mrs Larkin clutched her chest, the underarms of her pink frock darkened. Her body a trembling mass, she stared at the matriarch who could not stop Lexi's cry.

The muezzin called faithful for Maghrib, evening prayer.

Mrs Larkin closed her eyes for a brief moment. 'Please God…' she blubbered.

A few moments later, the matriarch made her way down the tree, with her wailing charge underarm. On reaching Mrs Larkin's veranda, she brushed the branches aside and disappeared out of sight.

'Stay here, Mr Larkin.' Mrs Larkin moved with stealth, but speed, back up the stairs to her place. She crept to the door of her baby's room. Through a gap in the door, she watched the matriarch put Lexi back in her cradle, cover her with the shawl, pucker her lips and kiss the curl on the top of her head.

I had heard this story so many times before, but now a veneer of something sacred and powerful stirs within me and I am trying to make sense of it, when Melvyn interrupts.

'How long will you be out of Calcutta, Gwen?'

I take a moment before answering. 'Maybe a week or two, not much longer than that, I have to get back to Australia. I'm here on a limited tourist visa.'

'That's your old sweeper, Pubna's living quarters,' Melvyn flicks his head in the direction of curlicues of smoke wafting from a slightly open door. Baby clothes are spread on its rooftop drying. 'His quarters were given away over two decades or more ago when he returned to his village permanently.'

'Poor man. When we were young girls, we were relentless in breaking off long pieces of sticks from his brooms to use as knitting needles,'

I lament as the image of the greying man with a wire-like frame rushes back to me.

It was Pubna's usual routine to collect his broom and sit upon his haunches on the veranda of our home, dip bread into his breakfast tea and eat. One morning, he was unusually early, without his broom and there was something distinctly different about his demeanour.

In a cheery voice, he greeted Mummy for the day.

'Why are you here so early? You know that you cannot sweep and wash the floors now, I have things to do inside.' Mummy never liked the help arriving earlier than their expected time. Not waiting for his response, Mummy brushed past him and into the house.

He finished his breakfast, then walked over and picked up a stick broom, shook it and put it back down. The two-foot-long sticks were a third of their usual length, but today he didn't complain. Manju, his fifteen-year-old nephew with muscles beneath ebony skin that glistened in the sun, had arrived from his village a few days earlier. He took up living quarters under the external stairwell of our double-storey building.

'Everything is fun,' Pubna muttered when he saw Manju run past him chasing the *bustee* children with handfuls of grey dust, taken from the coal *chula* that he had recently cleaned. 'Arses, Arses.' He showed off his new English words as he offered them ash to clean their teeth.

Empty mug in hand, Pubna wandered off to his *godown* and returned with all his belongings stuffed into a dhoti bundle. When he saw the *bikri* wallah, recycler man, on the veranda, with a flick-of-the-wrist, he threw his bundle on the floor, complaining bitterly at the length of time he would have to endure before getting Mummy's attention.

The recycler man sorted glassware, newspapers, cardboard and tin into separate piles, stopped to wrap and rewrap his head cloth as if in some sort of ceremony. He then proceeded to wipe his parched and deeply wrinkled hands on his stained shirt. Cross-legged he sat, with his legs hidden under his dhoti. Cracked feet peeped through as if they were in search of moisture. In a routine manner, he reached into his gunnysack, pulled out weighing scales, and put them down in front of himself. On one side of the scales, he loaded newspapers and cardboard, on the other a metal kilogram weight. He balanced the two sides equally by adding and taking away different size weights: a hundred gramss, two hundred, five hundred. When balanced, he tipped the recyclable paper load into a gunnysack.

The process resuming, this time with tin cans, metal bottle tops, a kettle, assorted aluminium pots and pans with holes in their bases. Next came tumblers, bottles and jars. A celluloid doll with one hand and some baby clothes were flung aside. An exchange of rupees to Mummy for all her recyclables brought a pleasing nod from Pubna. He rushed over to her, salvaging the discarded doll and baby clothes on his way, stuffing them into his dhoti bundle. The *bikri* wallah gathered his belongings and headed off to sell his recycling purchases.

'Memsahib, please,' Pubna called to Mummy.

'What is it, Pubna? Why aren't you sweeping?' Mummy asked, her attention diverted to the dhobi.

Within minutes of his arrival, an argument had erupted between the laundry man and Mummy over lost clothes, which he had taken a few days earlier.

Pubna, always smart enough not to let Mummy catch him idle while she was in a bad mood, picked up his quarter-sized broom and entered the house.

Within minutes, Mummy had ushered him back onto the veranda. 'Why were you hanging around the cot? Haven't I told you not to sweep under there when the little one is still asleep?'

'Sorry, memsahib, I was not disturbing, I was only taking a look at the *baccha*.'

'Stay outside,' said Mummy.

'Sorry, memsahib. Very, very, sorry, but I am needing to tell you something.'

'Not now. I'm busy.'

Parallel to and across from our place, Mrs Livingston, Melvyn's neighbour, pouted and flicked her dark hair back in a sweeping motion.

A baritone directly opposite her responded to her pouts from his balcony with a Jim Reeves rendition of 'He'll have to go'.

Mummy smirked.

The baritone set off a burst of energy for Pubna, who with robustness grabbed a broom and made a hasty retreat in the direction of the serenade.

On his return from the singer-sahib's house, he was laden with shirts. He smiled when he saw Mummy was occupied with the box wallahs. The string of men, each carrying a tin box on their heads, lowered the boxes onto the veranda to display their wares. Mummy bought sheets, towels, clothes, ribbons, sweets and cakes.

An hour or so later, when the vendors had departed, Pubna finally got Mummy's attention. 'Look, memsahib, upstairs sahib is giving me these things for my village people.' He unravelled a pile of men's shirts.

'Wait there,' Mummy ordered and disappeared.

Wobbling his head from side to side, Pubna fiddled with his dhoti bundle. He called Manju to join him in wait as he sat.

Ten minutes later, Mummy returned, arms laden with children's clothes, sheets and towels. Handing them to Manju, 'These are for you to take back to the village and that food too.' She pointed to a nearby wooden crate.

Pubna jumped to his feet. 'Memsahib, Manju is not going back to the village. I am. My wife is just having a *baccha*. Manju brought me the news.'

Lines formed on Mummy's forehead. 'But you have not been back to your village in three years!'

The greying Pubna patted his hair, bent down, picked up his full dhoti bundle, slung it over his shoulder. Puffing out his chest, 'But, my younger brother is there.' He trudged off.

At eight years old, lessons of sex or procreation would not have been imparted to me. Babies were delivered by stork overnight. Noticing the swollen belly of a pregnant woman was best not mentioned and definitely not questioned. Then, I didn't understand Mummy's raised eyebrows. Now, I suspect that Anglo-Indians were perhaps unaware that fraternal polyandry existed in ancient India.

Although outlawed in the mid-1950s, in modern-day India, in various, mostly remote, minority communities, a social tradition still exists, whereby the wife of the oldest brother in a family becomes 'common wife' to the younger brothers. The oldest brother is required to marry the woman first, the younger brothers then follow in marrying the same woman. However, they are not necessarily required to go through the marriage ritual in order to be deemed co-husbands to her. The older brother is not permitted to take the wife of a younger brother.

In the compound, children are at play, servants are entering and exiting homes in which they are employed. I scan the servant women, and for a moment consider, are they a common wife?

'Gwen, on your return, we could spend a few days in the city and take in some old Calcutta sights. Have a think about what takes your fancy,' says Melvyn.

'Thanks, Melvyn. That's nice of you to offer. On my list of places to visit are my old school, my father's place of work and a trip to Alipore Zoo…'

Distracted by primary school age girls cowering in a corner, I excuse myself and run over to check if they are okay. The oldest of the three children holds a finger over her lips. I then realise that I almost interrupted a game of hide and seek. Embarrassed, I leave them alone.

My head fills with the memory of the many times in my Indian childhood when I huddled together with my brother and sisters for comfort during violent racial clashes.

At Indian Independence, when British India was partitioned, India remained with its majority Hindu regions. The north-western fringes of India became West Pakistan, and the north-eastern fringes, a few hundred kilometres away from the border of Calcutta, the place of my family home, became East Pakistan (now Bangladesh). Two non-bordering regions of Muslim majorities became Pakistan. East and West Pakistan were geographically divided by India. The ongoing unrest over divisions of land, rivers and people diminished India's relationships with Pakistan and the communities who had since moved to East Pakistan from India.

India's princely states on the borders were not included as British India and as such were not in the British-commissioned report for partition. These states were left to decide which divided country they wanted to align with – India or Pakistan. Most princely states made affable arrangements, but territorial conflict arose in India's north, with both countries claiming the region of Kashmir. India gained control over two-thirds in the southern half of Kashmir, which was organised as Jammu-Kashmir. Pakistan gained the other third. This split created ongoing conflict between the two countries.

6

I was nine years old in 1964, when one of these tensions left an indelible mark on my memory. And it would be a catalyst for my family leaving India in the years to come.

Following the disappearance of a precious relic from a mosque in Srinagar, capital of the Indian-held area of the disputed state of Jammu and Kashmir, anti-Hindu riots broke out. Retaliation against Muslims by Hindus erupted and continued in the rural areas of the state of West Bengal and spread to the city of Calcutta and other nearby districts.

One afternoon following a night of such riots, Catherine took Hannah and me to buy rationed bread. Outside the pink and green mosque, bodies were strewn – still, grey faces, shirts stained in dried blood, unblinking eyes wide open, gazing skyward. Flies, with wings in full oscillation, fluttered around open mouths. Rigor mortis had set in. My knees knocked and my stomach heaved. The *modi* had been looted. Grains, flour, vegetables, spices spilled onto the streets. Police had threatened to shoot bystanders in the legs if they did not comply with the curfew hours set down. Without hesitation, the three of us ran home. No bread.

The previous night, kerosene fumes and voices from the outdoors crept under the doors and mingled with our bedtime prayers, 'As-it-was-in-the-beginning-is-now-and-ever-shall-be-world-without-end.'

A double-brick six-foot-high wall was all that separated us from a lane that ran the length of the back of our house. Hundreds of feet pounded, metal chains clanged and guns fired as political protesters raged, shouting slogans in a continuous rhythm as if in mantra, but we were unable make them out. Dogs picking up on their trail howled in unison through the night.

Daddy wasn't home from work and, before Mummy could stop us, Hannah and I peeped through the timber shutters of the back door. Lighted torches shone into our backyard turning it into a fiery sea. Nana lit a kerosene lamp. Mummy turned off the lights and rang a neighbour.

'Children, you have to go to stay in the Beggs' place tonight. It will be safer there. They are higher up.'

Within minutes, Nana gathered the youngest four children together and we stole out of our front door. I brought There-There, my fabric doll in one hand and held Hannah's hand with the other. Carrying the coolness of the night air on our shoulders, we stayed close to the wall like Mummy had instructed. Enveloped in the pitch-blackness of night, we reached the stairwell to the Beggs' house. I let go of Hannah's hand and scrambled my way upstairs, almost on my hands and knees. It was the easiest way for me to climb upward in the dark.

A torch shone through the air, giving faint and momentary light, landing with a thud in the front yard. My heart thumped like elephants on a rampage. My screams must have scared my legs, they flopped like rags and disappeared from under me. I slid down a few steps and lost my grip on my doll. She vanished into the darkness. Hannah scampered down after me, placed a hand over my mouth and pulled me up with her other. Hot tears streamed down my face and my stomach went to mush.

'There-There,' I whimpered.

'You can get her in the morning,' said the soft but stern voice of Mrs Begg, who appeared on the stairwell.

'I want…need her now.'

'Not now, Gwen.' An adult hand stroked my back.

When we reached Mrs Begg's veranda, she showed us to her front door and helped us in. Nana settled us down and assured me that she would find my toy. She gave the sigh that usually meant she was drained of energy. Mummy said she sighed like that because she missed our Auntie Myrtle, who disappeared when she was fifteen. Ran away. I never met my Auntie Myrtle and Daddy never spoke openly about his sister.

The Beggs had made a field bed on their drawing room floor with blankets. At first, the four of us children stuck together like magnets.

But, after some time, although we were still afraid, Nelson said, 'Let's pretend that we are camping outdoors, listening to the ocean, like when we visit our cousins in Madras.'

We settled down, pretending to see stars and the man in the moon.

Growing up, it was usual, during the long hot summer school holidays, for Mummy and the four younger children to visit our relatives in the south of India, Madras. We spent whole days at the beach, followed by kite-flying in the evening. At night, our Auntie Merlyn, Mummy's oldest sister, never objected to us taking beds into the quarter-acre backyard to gaze at the stars and be fanned by the sea breezes. It was conditional that we set up close to the house and keep our distance from the well that was tucked into one corner of the backyard. Lush mango trees, laden with fruit, sprawled over the rest of the area.

Three of the many cousins, who were closer in age to Nelson, Hannah and me, joined us outdoors. The two boys in the group had a bed of their own, while the four girls squashed into one four-poster bed. One night, thunder rumbled and bolts of lightning zipped across the sky, creating a luminous and mystical light show, forcing a hasty retreat indoors. We set up both beds in the one room, side by side so that we could all stay together. Cousin Bess hastened to caution us that the rooms were haunted.

In an instant, Hannah, Nelson and I jumped up, stripped the sheets off the bed and chased her. 'Coming to get you.'

Thunder clapped overhead.

'Stop, it is not a joke. A woman once drowned in the well in the backyard. She possessed me. I thrashed with pain and fever and Mummy said my face turned blue and I talked in the drowned woman's voice,' said Bess.

Laura, her sister defended her. 'Don't tease. She is telling the truth. The priest had to be called to exorcise her.'

The priest had exercised Bess too much, I thought. Her bones poked through her skin.

We created a noise to compete with the thunder that awakened Auntie Merlyn. She rushed into the room, long grey hair flying, struggling to push her bony arms into the sleeves of her dressing gown.

Bess tattled on us. 'Mum, they don't believe me.'

Auntie Merlyn, a staunch Catholic, forced us into prayer at every opportunity. Our mother was religious too, but nothing in comparison to her older sister.

'My poor Bess, she was stricken.' Auntie made the sign of the cross. 'She's only been better for a few weeks before your visit. You three will need to say a decade of the rosary for teasing Bess and another one to ward off bad spirits, then please go straight to bed,' she said in her holiest voice, and tucked Bess back into bed.

Nelson, Hannah and I raced through the prescribed two decades of the rosary, while we remade beds and jumped in, bellowing, 'Amen, almond, all right.'

The next day, as soon as my mother arrived, I bolted to her side and reported that Bess had been exorcised.

Mummy held her breath, then her face became as white as the inside flesh of a coconut that we had not long ago eaten. 'Gwen, get packed, you will have to stay with Daddy and me from now on.'

That would be in her brother's house, which was far away from all the fun.

'Why should I be the only one to go?' I howled.

'Because I said so.'

Of course, I rummaged up a heartbroken wail. Mummy drew me into her, while talking to her sister. I could not hear their conversation, because I kept up my loud and pitiful cry. Soon, the household altar was awash with flickering candles. Holy water was sprinkled around the rooms and we were all given a good sprinkle too, though I was almost given a full shower. Damp and hoarse on bended knees, we were swept into prayer, after which I was allowed to stay.

At sunset that evening, again in the backyard, we finished up a game of cricket. Everyone had gone indoors, when I decided to pluck a few ripe mangoes.

A woman with long dark hair, swinging a bucket, walked down to the well.

'Hello, I'm Gwen,' I called.

Inside the dining room, I unloaded a skirt full of mangoes into the fruit bowl and washed up in readiness for dinner. South Indian food of *dosa* was being prepared from fermented rice and lentils – a paper-thin, wafer-like crêpe cooked on a hot griddle. With potato rolled at its centre, it is eaten with coconut chutney and sambal, gravy with vegetables. Seated at the table, we said Grace. The warmth of the day had warmed the mangoes and their scent flooded the room.

Being from West Bengal, we were unaccustomed to eating food from the south and it took some thought as how to navigate these large crêpes with fingers, the traditional way to eat them. The dinner table was unusually quiet with some concentration required to master the new art of eating the speciality of the region. Gravy dripping like a leaking tap reminded me of the lady with a bucket heading to the well.

'Auntie, a lady was going down to the well when I was collecting mangoes. Should I let her know dinner is served?'

Auntie choked on her crêpe and turned as white as the rice it had been cooked from. Lifting her glass, she gulped water to help wash down the stuck food, I guessed. Dinner was brought to an instant halt and we were ordered to kneel at the altar.

Mummy must have been called, because she arrived in the middle of prayers. She rubbed her forehead, as if she were trying to soothe a headache. I'm sure my crying didn't help her pain.

She carried me to the car and the whole way back to her brother's house I was kicking and screaming. 'I am sorry, Gwen. I do not know what to do.'

'Let me stay,' I bawled.

'I cannot let you stay. I am sorry.'

It was at times like this that I could not make sense of my mother. She would not give me a reason for constantly hovering over me or making me come indoors before sunset.

Although that was a memory from a long time ago, lying on the Beggs' floor and recalling that woman was so immediate that I let out an earth-shattering cry, 'I want to stay!'

A torch waved and a sliver of light cut across my face. Mrs Begg rushed over, talking into her hands, 'You can stay, dear, but please be quiet.'

My thoughts ceased and I was reminded that I was on the Beggs' floor. The light went out and I sensed Mrs Begg crouch beside me.

At intervals, Mr Begg went to the window facing the backyard and lifted the shutters, reporting, 'Rioters are still running in hordes down the lane, but they are no longer throwing kerosene torches over the wall. The ones already there are fading. Christians have nothing to fear.'

My dread hung like a thick branch ready to drop. I didn't know what a Christian was. I was Catholic. I didn't know if we were safe or not.

Hannah suggested we pray a litany: 'Holy Mother of God – pray for us, angels and saints – pray for us, pray for us, for us.'

We said it in hushed tones all night. Sometimes, we got so quiet I wondered if Heaven even knew that we were praying and would protect us.

Throughout the night, shouts and slogans from the rioters mingled with our prayers. In the distance, catchphrases swirled and exploding sounds quaked.

'That's a bomb going off. Stay quiet, we don't want the rioters to know that we are here,' said Mrs Begg.

That was enough to make me jump up and cross my legs. 'I need to do *sou-sou*.'

'Can you wait, Gwen?'

'No, auntie, I have to go now.'

The torch went on, and Mrs Begg held a finger to her lips the entire way to the bathroom. 'Be quiet, dear,' she said.

I tried hard to be as quiet as one can with these things, but I didn't think that the rioters were interested in my bathroom sounds. I didn't understand why we had to be quiet and turn the lights off. After all, they were much noisier than we were and they knew that people lived here. Wouldn't turning the lights off tell the rioters that these homes had no one in them and were free to loot? I was certain it was crazy but I was such a scaredy cat, I said nothing.

Back on the floor, stillness and fear sifted together deep inside me. Darkness cocooned and the shapes of people I had never known came and whispered, 'Be still, all will be well.' Some even touched me on the head, the arm.

I closed my eyes and wished for There-There. I missed her softness, her smell. Crying, I buried my face in the pillow.

When I opened my eyes, I wasn't in my own bed or even in my own house.

Mr and Mrs Begg were fussing, 'Wash your face, brush your teeth, we've made porridge, toast and tea.'

The loud sounds from the previous night were gone. The chickens clucked, dogs snapped and children played in the compound.

On my way home down the stairs, I found my doll with her head scrunched against the wall. She was very cold. I gave her a big hug and, when I got home, I wrapped my handkerchief around her shoulders. The Muslim servants did not show up for work.

Later that morning, Daddy came home with a copy of the morning's newspaper tucked under his arm. He had been supervising at the press all night.

Sister Mary spread the paper on the table. 'Hindu–Muslim Riots in Calcutta...' she said.

In the background, on the radio, *Askashvani Calcutta's* signature tune alerted us to the news bulletin. Mummy turned up the crackling volume. Mary rested a palm on either end of the paper.

Mummy then gave us a news report of her own. '...a hundred people have been killed and two hundred cases of arson have been reported. Over seven thousand people have been arrested and four hundred and thirty-eight injured in the clashes. Several incidents of stabbing and bombings have occurred, properties are being looted and burned. Two rubber factories have been set on fire along with a number of shops and dwellings.'

I covered my ears, but I could still hear.

'The Indian government has claimed that the trouble in Calcutta has taken a huge toll of life. Curfew has been declared for the next twenty-four hours. No buses and trams will be operating and most markets and shops will remain shut. Educational institutions will also remain closed. The armed forces and police were given orders by the government – shoot to kill.'

Mummy, Daddy and Mary were talking about how seventy thousand people had fled their homes in the city and fifty-five thousand were thought to be sleeping in the open air, under army protection. Relief organisations were struggling to provide food, water and sanitation to large groups of refugees. Electrical shops were pillaged. Milk, bread, flour and rice were in short supply and these commodities would be rationed over the next few weeks.

In the days that followed, we witnessed bloodstains being washed away from streets and walls. Businesses that had been burned or looted were undertaking cleaning and repairs on their premises. Shops partially opened their doors or a small window to sell goods at intervals during the day and varied operational times.

'Anglo-Indians were never targeted during these outbreaks, but caution had to be taken not to get in the crossfire,' said Daddy. But Daddy's sombre mood that day gave us clues as to his concern for our safety and would have been a contributing factor in his and Mummy's decision to leave India permanently.

Melvyn and I continue walking in the compound, my mind now fresh with memories of these disturbances. 'Do you still have riots, Melvyn?'

'Not really, Gwen. Things are more tempered these days.'

I reflected on some previous situations when I lived in India, and how we had grown used to insurgence. Although a witness to some atrocities, now, I cannot imagine these soft-spoken, kind, generous Indians that I had been in contact with during my travels as being capable of revolting.

The tenderness of the women nursing babies is touching. Their smiles remind me of the joy the new arrival in our family brought in that year of racial riots, but there were also departures. It is said that as a new generation arrives, another departs.

7

Following the tumultuous period that the riots created in Calcutta, life was getting back to normal, as we knew it. Patricia's husband had been seconded to work on a ship in Europe and she returned temporarily to live with us. Months after her husband had gone, Patricia's slender figure began to change. In the autumn of 1964, she welcomed a son, Winston. There was great celebration for the new arrival, especially from the grandparents and great-grandmother Nana, who had turned seventy-two. I was now an auntie.

In May of the following year, on my tenth birthday, Mummy was huddled beside Nana's bed, in the same way she had done for many months now. The family had forgotten my birthday. I felt upset and wanted to remind them but it would be too unkind to interrupt Mummy and the others, who had been waiting from early that morning for a doctor to visit Nana. In the evening, when they remembered that it was my birthday, it was too late to do anything anyway and everyone at home remained as quiet as possible, so not as to disrupt Nana. Catherine took me to her friend's house, who also had a birthday. Estelle let me share cutting her birthday cake. There were only grown-ups at the party and it was uninteresting, but I was happy to have cake.

When we returned, our house was as quiet as a graveyard. Mummy was in her bed, asleep. Mary sat beside Nana's bed. Catherine and I crept around, getting ready for bed.

The next day turned out to be a scorcher. School had closed for the long hot break. Patricia made a trip to the bank and replenished crisp ten- and twenty-rupee notes as if she were replenishing flowers in an open bowl that she kept on her dresser since her husband's departure.

There would be no holiday to the beach this summer. Nana was still unwell and Mummy was exhausted from the constant vigil of caring for her. She accepted assistance from Catherine and Mary, who took turns to sit beside Nana day and night. Catherine usually fell asleep during her shift and was taken off that duty.

A couple of weeks later, on a morning when Daddy was leaving for work, he stopped for a minute beneath the family altar at the consecrated picture of the Sacred Heart of Jesus, with a candle flickering in a red glass candleholder. 'June second, feast of the Sacred Heart,' he said.

In my adult life, I found out that it was an auspicious day for Nana, who had had that picture consecrated by a Catholic bishop almost half a century earlier, in keeping with a promise that she had made to the Sacred Heart. Nana, an Anglican converted to Catholicism, believed it was her faith and prayers that enabled her to conceive a child, my father.

Daddy, Mary and Catherine left together for work. Winston was now nine months old. I hoisted him on my hip and took him outdoors to see them off, enjoying the final coolness that the day would offer. He chuckled as I rocked him until we both laughed hysterically, each triggered by the other.

After half an hour or so, I was overcome with the fragrance of lilies. I looked around but there were no flowers to be seen. The overpowering scent crept into my chest, to the point of leaving me breathless. Frightened, my laughter ceased and I stood still. Winston gave one of his baby grunts and wriggled his legs as if to kick-start me again, but I remained motionless.

Patricia rushed towards us, eyes red and swollen. She wrapped her arms around Winston and me. Pressed hard and then stepped back. She took the baby from me, kissed his head, looked at me and stroked mine. 'Nana's gone,' she said.

'Gone where?'

'To Jesus.'

'How could she? She's sick in bed and can't walk. Besides, we didn't see her go past us.'

Patricia's eyes filled with tears. 'We can't see someone when they go to Jesus. We just know that they do.'

'Can we go inside?' I asked, curious to see if Nana's bed was empty.

'No, we have to stay outside for now.'

'Why?' My question went unheeded.

Patricia and I wiped perspiration off our foreheads as we sat on recliners in the shade of the veranda. Patricia dabbed her eyes every now and then.

'Why are you crying?' I asked.

'Nana,' she muttered.

I didn't understand why she should cry about that. Wouldn't it be good to be with Jesus?

Ayah brought us two tall glasses of *nimbu pani*, a popular summer thirst quencher, freshly squeezed lemon juice, cool water, salt or sugar, usually salt in the summer months. She gave Winston a rusk, which he stuck in his mouth as if he had been starved forever.

Daddy came home from work, brushing past us in a hurry. He was pale and sombre. Mary arrived shortly after he did, with the family doctor a few paces behind. The doctor's black bag was open, its contents almost spilling out. They too rushed past as if we didn't exist.

I watched the front door of our house intently for a few minutes and then settled back in my chair. Patricia picked up her drink. I copied her in taking small sips.

After around twenty minutes or so, doctor and Daddy were at the front door. They talked for a short time, then shook their heads. In anticipation of what they would do next, I gulped down my drink. Finally, the doctor gave Daddy a firm pat on his shoulder and shook his hand. When he passed us, his eyebrows darted upward from his black rimmed spectacles, scrunching his forehead into deep furrows.

Anxious to find out what was going on indoors, 'Patricia, I need to go.' I crossed my legs.

Instead, Patricia took me to a neighbour's house. Mrs Atkins was all smiles. Patricia whispered something to her. Her smile vanished and she showed me to the bathroom. On my return, she was making ridiculous faces at Winston and talking to Patricia in a very soft tone.

'What to do? It's not in our control,' she said. And, jumping back into life, 'I've made brown stew. Stay for lunch. I will boil up a pot of rice…'

'Thanks for the offer. The family will not eat meat today, because of the…'

Mrs Atkins nodded. 'I understand.'

I wished I did.

We returned to our veranda. Winston whimpered, Patricia left him with me and went indoors to get him something to eat. A few minutes later, she returned with a bowl filled with a creamy mixture. It looked bland, but the whinger child could hardly wait for it. Patricia picked up a spoonful of the mixture and mimicked a plane flying around then lowered the spoon into his open mouth, for a landing. He slurped up the disgusting mixture and clapped his hands.

Nelson and Hannah returned from their outing.

I wanted to be the bearer of the sad news. 'Nana has gone to Jesus. We need to stay outdoors.' The words rushed out.

Hannah appeared to not be moved one way or the other, but Nelson looked away and pulled a handkerchief from his pocket. Patricia gave them her miserable look, while patting each one on the shoulder.

Patricia asked the three of us to remain where we were while she took Winston indoors to put him down for a rest. Ayah brought us *piajus,* an Indian snack of potatoes, onions and carrot slices, dipped in chickpea batter and fried. We dipped the cooked pieces in mango chutney and devoured the entire serving in minutes.

A couple of hours passed before we were allowed inside our house. The drawing room had its furniture pushed back against the walls. Nana was lying on a makeshift bed in the middle of the room, covered with a sheet that draped all the way to the floor. Her silvery hair was neatly parted down one side, the way she usually wore it with a bobby clip that held it off her face. Her eyes were closed, and she had a very stiff smile. One of Daddy's large white handkerchiefs looped from under her chin to the top of her head and tied in a neat bow. At either side of the bedhead, there were lighted candles and tall empty vases.

I was surprised to see Nana. Didn't she go to Jesus?

An hour or so later, two men delivered blocks of ice in metal buckets. One of them lifted the draped sheets and pushed the buckets underneath. From his market shop, Mali, the florist, brought white lilies, placed them in the empty vases, added water. Their fragrance spread. Mummy, prayer book in hand, sat weeping beside Nana's bed.

Before long, the clack-clack-clack of rosary beads heralded the arrival of Father Picachy, the parish priest. He nodded to everyone and looked at Daddy and Mummy. 'She's in God's care now,' he said fiddling in a pocket of his black cassock. Clack-clack, the beads tolled as he pulled a small black bag from within, extracting two bottles – holy water and holy oil. He put them down on the temporary altar, lined with a white cotton crocheted cloth. Turning the gold trim pages in his prayer book back and forth, he marked a couple of pages with silver satin ribbons.

The family were called to kneel around 'the body' as he now referred to Nana.

After each section of prayer, he invited us to join him and say, 'May she rest in peace.'

I didn't know why he wanted us to say that. She already looked very peaceful.

Father put a thumb over the mouth of the bottle with oil and tipped it up. He pulled back the top of Nana's covering, tucked his hand inside the top of her frock, anointed her chest and made a sign of the cross on her throat, lips, eyes and ears with his oily thumb. He covered her without care. 'Let's pray for the deceased,' he said, and sprinkled 'the body' and everyone in the room, with holy water.

Mummy had bags under her eyes and dark circles too. Her hands shook when she handed father an envelope. He shoved it into his pocket without even looking at it or her. Mummy then tidied the sheet over 'the body'.

Men in black measured 'the body', talked to Daddy then left. 'The body' stayed in the drawing room overnight. The usual four had to once again camp at Mr and Mrs Begg's place.

The next morning when we came home, everything was exactly as we had left it the previous night, except that there were candles all around Nana's makeshift bed, and the adults had dark circles around their eyes.

Father Picachy returned at ten o'clock and said more prayers. Neighbours, family friends and colleagues from Daddy's work, and other people that I didn't recognise, came with flowers and food. Everyone was dressed in black except for the family's younger children, who wore their best coloured, going-out clothes. The family circled 'the body' and then stood solemnly with hands clasped in front.

Neighbours and friends stood as if they had been set in concrete. Servants maintained their respect, watching at a distance from the veranda.

The men in black returned with a long black box. They laid it on Daddy's wooden workhorse, alongside Nana's makeshift bed and removed its lid with a shiny gold crucifix fixed to it. They lifted 'the body' into it, settled the bedding within and nailed it shut. Family members were invited to place a white lily on top. People wept when Daddy helped the men in black lift the box and carry it away.

Mrs Begg said, 'Children don't go to funerals.'

Nelson, Hannah, Alison and I stayed home with Ayah. Everyone else followed the black box.

The members of our family, who went to the funeral, returned a few hours later. They never spoke to us or touched anything before they washed their face and hands. The drawing room went back to its usual look and everyone was sorrowful. The sadness of Nana's body leaving in a black box and not fully understanding how she went to Jesus at the same time remained with me until I grew older and understood more about death.

A few months after Nana's death, Daddy bought a big bottle-green Dodge, with luxury seats and air conditioning. We moved to a new residence, in the locality of Beck Began. It was in a block of six apartments, with a semicircular balcony that served as the family photo spot. Also, it provided views across the neighbourhood. It is the same area in which I now stay with Diana and is an urgent reminder that I must head back. I bid Melvyn farewell, assuring him that I will phone him on my return from travels around the country.

'Hello, Diana. I'm back,' I call through the security door as I enter.

'How was your day with Melvyn?'

'It was a grand day. We shared many fond memories. We didn't get through the whole compound, so we agreed to catch up after my sojourn around the country.'

Diana draws a blank look, as if it is the first time that she has heard that I am going elsewhere, even though I had told her the day I booked my flight and have reminded her several times since.

'When will you go?'

'Tomorrow.'

'Did you book a driver to take you to the airport? I don't drive, you know.'

Even if she did drive, she doesn't own a car or have a licence, so I am baffled.

'Yes thanks, Diana. It is the same driver who brought me to your place when I first arrived. I've called him today to confirm. I'll be back in a week or two. I hope that's not an inconvenience.'

'Not at all. I do not plan on going anywhere.' Diana's cheery smile vanishes, and she feverishly tugs on her sleeve.

I suspect she is uncomfortable with me travelling around India solo. I decide not to be drawn into her discomfort, whatever that may be. It is very late afternoon and I offer the excuse of packing bags for my forthcoming trip and return to my room.

I pack lightly, flick the overhead fan on and crash on the bed. Staring up at the ceiling, I watch the fan's blades gather momentum. In my half sleep, their whirr-whirr magnifies in my ears.

8

The whirr, whirr, whirring of overhead fans comforted me most nights during my childhood. Hannah and I shared a double bed. Often for me, sleep didn't come easily and through the blackness I stared towards the ceiling. Sometimes, people-shapes floated above or sat beside me. I'd squeeze my eyes tight and pull the sheets over my head. Daddy had a suggestion for when we couldn't sleep. In my mind's eye, I visualised a mound of rice – then watched an ant take a grain from it and run back to its hole. Usually, that trick worked.

One night, following many hundreds of ants scurrying to their holes, I was still awake when the rooster next door gave his shrill morning call. I opened an eye, caught the light creeping under the door as if it were a thief and I remembered the time when our bungalow had been robbed.

Our entire family had been anaesthetised. Overnight, rags doused in chloroform were shoved through barred windows. When we awoke, it was late morning, and a strange odour lingered in the air. Mummy and Daddy moved as if they were sleepwalking. When I saw them near my bed, I called out, but the words did not come out. My mind felt heavy and scattered like clouds. My lips were tight and blistered, and my throat dry. Through my foggy mind, I could hear Ayah's distant voice, but her words were garbled. She was offering Mummy and Daddy something in tumblers.

A short time later, the kettle whistled to a boil and that shocked my numb body and brain back to some normality. I went to the dining room, where family members looked pale and zombie-like. Ayah told us she had been knocking on the front door for fifteen minutes or more since her arrival at six o'clock. Daddy, cup of tea in hand, carried out an inspection, noting that the bathroom window's bars had been bent apart and the glass pane shattered. The back door had been opened from the inside. Silverware was missing, along with wallets, cash from handbags. The tops of dressers and drawers had been emptied of gold bracelets, emerald and ruby rings, jewellery boxes laid bare.

For India's poverty-stricken, with no social security benefits, theft is a means of survival. India's caste system forbids lower castes to have contact with higher castes, thus keeping lower castes in an isolated existence of untouchability and structural poverty.

Eighteenth-century India, a country of manufacturing and agriculture, exported looms to Asia and Europe. Under British rule, the East India Company forced land onto unskilled farming people. This was exclusively instigated for the purpose of collecting land tax from the encumbered owners. The unskilled farmers borrowed from moneylenders to purchase the lands. Fuelled by fraud and extortion, the lenders kept tillers of the soil and payers of taxed, uncultivated land indebted to them – becoming the borrowers' greatest curse.

Half of the taxes collected in India was remitted annually to Great Britain. Skilled Indians were discouraged by the East India Company from manufacture. Instead, they were encouraged and instructed in the production of raw materials to facilitate manufacture in Great Britain. Indian artisans were forced into the employment of the company's factories. Tariffs were placed on community weavers and villages. Indian-manufactured silk and cotton goods had tariffs imposed on them. English imports into India of the same items attracted minimal or no tariff, plunging lower-caste Indians into further debt.

Following the burglary, the neighbourhood agreed that calling the police was the most useless thing to do. You had to learn how to protect your own home and belongings. At night, barking dogs were the security alert to strangers or prowlers lurking around.

One night, when Daddy was still awake, he saw a thief bending apart the bars on a window with his crowbar. When the burglar put his hand through the bars, Daddy whacked it with his cricket bat. There was a loud cry as the thief ran away, not stopping for his crowbar.

But that was not a permanent deterrent. Thieves returned time and time again, with their bodies covered in oil, to enable them to slip away if they were grabbed. After our burglary, Mummy and Daddy decided to shut and bolt all the windows and doors overnight.

My forthcoming trip to Varanasi excites me. Venturing there would once have been frowned upon. Anglo-Indians didn't make trips to witness Arti, the sacred Hindu fire ceremony on the holy Ganges River. I toss and turn with excitement. Over and over, I pray for sleep and feel my eyes growing heavy, when I hear dogs barking in unison. I feel as if I am entering a bad dream. My heart pounds, I pull the sheets over my head and wait in anticipation for the sound of breaking glass, and a well-oiled hand to reach in.

Disturbed, hours later I am still awake. I roll out my yoga mat – it is my usual early morning routine, albeit considerably earlier today. I stretch my limbs, centring on my breath and within minutes my apprehension subsides. In preparation for the day, I include warrior pose in my practice. I sit in meditation for an hour, before replacing the mat in its travel bag. I don't want to disturb Diana by wandering around the house, so I lie on my made bed and gather thoughts of my upcoming travels. I drift off, then startle awake when I hear doors being unbolted. The sound of our front door being unbolted was my cue, as a child, to inch out of bed. In an instant, I am transported back to the morning following my fifth birthday.

In the coolness of the compound, I sat on the front veranda steps of our bungalow. With my nightdress pulled over my knees, I ran a finger around the soft, warm, swollen cotton flowers that Mummy had embroidered. I brushed curls off my face and rubbed sleep from my eyes.

Jumadhars arrived from the early hours of the morning, like chimney sweeps, brooms in hand, each waiting to begin their daily sweeper duties, which did not include fireplaces. Ayahs disappeared into various households, only to reappear a short time later on verandas, rice sieves in hand. Singing sweet songs, they picked unwanted bits of grit or glass from raw rice and threw it to the mud.

Tuk-tuk-tuk, a mother hen strutted around with her chickens scratching up the dirt, she stuck her beak in and drew out a long, reddish-pink earthworm. From her beak, the ends of its body wriggled like tentacles. She thrashed it around until it broke into manageable pieces and shared them amongst her little ones.

I looked down at the powdered muck under my bare feet and heard Nana's voice in my head. 'Put your shoes on. How many times do I have to tell you children not to go barefoot in the mud? You will get worms.'

Without shoes, I kicked up dust storms. Each rise and fall of the hazy whirl created a pattern of its own. The swirls made me think about the new sweeper boy, Manju, who since his arrival often created a whirlwind, chasing younger children in the dirt. I glanced towards his makeshift door under the stairwell. His privacy curtain, an old dhoti strung over a thick rope, was undisturbed.

'Hello, my child.' I heard a man's voice.

I faced an old man sitting beside me, dressed in blue and white striped pyjamas. His creased skin was like crêpe paper and as white as milk. Strands of silvery hair swept across his shining skull. Round, black-framed spectacles hung off the end of his nose.

'Hello Uncle.'

'I saw that you had one of those nice Nahoum's cakes for your birthday party yesterday.'

'Yes, Uncle. A maypole cake.'

'Did you like your birthday presents? You got a doll's house.'

'How do you know? You were not at my party, Uncle.' I looked away, fingernails between my teeth.

'Oh, I see lots of things. I am sure you will have fun with that doll's house.' He tapped the steps gently, without sound.

I looked away to give myself time to consider if I should tell him that the doll's house had lights that turned on and off. When I looked back seconds later, he was gone.

Utensils clanging in Diana's kitchen are sufficient to tell me she is awake. The driver will soon be here for my ride to the airport.

I freshen up and head to the kitchen, poke my head in. 'Good morning, Diana.'

'Sorry if I disturbed you, Gwen. I was trying to get something ready for you to eat before you leave.'

'Not at all. That's very kind of you to organise breakfast, but a tea will do me fine. I can get something at the airport, I'll have plenty of time.'

'Nonsense, you must have something proper before you go.'

Diana is not in need of help, and I decide to collect my bag and my trusty yoga mat. As the waft of porridge slinks under my bedroom door, I do a double-check that my passport is packed.

The smell of porridge cooking takes me back to the morning that the old man with round glasses had visited me on the steps outdoors. Daddy had an early start and was saying his goodbyes for the day. I waved him off and readied myself to join everyone at the table. Alison, our two-year-old, was missing for breakfast. She had kept everyone up through the night crying and she was probably asleep now that we were all awake.

Shortly after Daddy had left for work, Mummy led Grace, 'Bless us O Lord, and these thy gifts, which through thy bounty we are about to receive through Christ our L—'

The front door opened again. Ayah rushed into the dining room, head and face concealed with the end of her sari, only revealing eyes, filled with gloom. It was customary for her to cover her head when Daddy was around – a tradition of her community, where women covered their head in the presence of a male who did not belong in their family.

'Memsahib, memsahib, memsahib,' she puffed, struggling to draw breath.

'What is it?' asked Mummy.

'Bad thing, bad thing, memsahib.'

'What bad thing?'

'Please, memsahib, come quick.' She rushed away.

Mummy excused herself from the table, closing the dining room door behind her. Moments later, the front door, timber with a glass pane, opened and slammed shut.

Older sister Mary completed grace, and together we said, 'Amen.' With porridge eaten, we were being served eggs on toast, when Mummy, Daddy and Ayah returned, looking concerned. Ayah stacked up the used bowls and plates as if she were a robot. Mummy collapsed into a chair.

Daddy had deep creases on his forehead. He paced the floor for a few minutes then stopped abruptly. 'Children, please don't go out the front today. Play in the backyard,' he said.

Although we were surprised to see Daddy there, no one questioned it.

'Lovie,' he turned to Mummy, 'I will take care of it.' With that, he left.

Hannah and I looked at each other. We knew each other's thoughts. An action plan had to be put in place, to find out what Daddy would take care of and why we were not allowed out the front. Mummy tried to act as if everything was normal and began supervising the servants in their daily jobs. Hannah and I checked on everyone who was left at home. Mary was reading. Nelson was building with Meccano. It was his favourite school holiday pastime – that is, when he wasn't inventing gadgets or blowing up the bathroom with a chemical compound that he had created with his chemistry set. Catherine was studying or flipping through fashion magazines. Either way, she would not be checking on us.

With the coast clear, Hannah and I bolted into the drawing room.

We were almost the same height. If I stood on her shoulders, together we could probably reach the glass panel on the front door, but that would not work. I considered the glass to be 'a hundred million feet high up'.

'Could be,' said Hannah.

'How are we going to find out what's going on if we can't look outside?' I asked.

'I know what to do,' said Hannah.

Hannah could always be relied on knowing what to do. Out on the back veranda, we found an empty wooden crate. Checking that we would not get caught, we carried it over to the front door and jumped up onto it. The glass panel was still too high up. We needed another plan. A dining chair in the nearby room was perfect. Carefully, and without sound, we lifted it onto the crate.

'Hold the chair steady for me,' said Hannah and she climbed up, looked through the pane. 'The ayahs have their faces covered. Daddy must still be around,' said Hannah. 'Wait. Everyone keeps looking under the stairwell and pulling funny faces.'

'Give me a look,' I said.

'Not yet.'

'I want to look, let me, let me.'

'Okay, but you have to be quick.' Hannah scaled down.

I climbed onto the box. My legs shook as if they were experiencing an earthquake. I lay my body over the chair and finally lifted myself up, all this done with my eyes firmly closed, until I could stand up.

Daddy was talking to a man wearing a white skullcap, dhoti and kurta. The man had bushy greying eyebrows and sunken eyes. Manju stood next to them and did not look his usual glossy self. The man talking to Daddy was pointing under the stairwell and shaking his head.

'Hurry up,' said Hannah.

'It's my turn,' I said, and watched Daddy open his wallet and give the man who he was talking to a bunch of rupees.

The man raised a hand to his forehead. I knew that meant he was saying thank you.

'Hannah, Daddy is leaving and Manju looks sad. Why do you think he is holding his head in his hands?' I asked.

'Manju is not there. I think something has happened to him.'

'Yes, he is. You must have seen him. I just did.'

'He is not. Give me another look.'

I began to climb down and realised that Hannah was nearly all the way up. We stood beside each other.

'Manju is not there. I can't see him,' she said.

'Yes, he is.'

'You're imagining things.'

'Am not.' By this time, I was quivering like a scared mouse that had caught sight of Topsy, our tabby cat.

'Stop shaking,' said Hannah. She put her arm around my shoulders.

'Big day.' Diana slinks an arm around my shoulders.

I'm surprised, considering I don't think she approves of my future travels and probably thinks I should not be contaminating my precious British heritage by visiting other religious places in India. I am in no mood to have this discussion with her.

'I've never been to Delhi and I look forward to walking in my father's footsteps,' I said.

'That surprises me. I thought your family would all have been to Delhi.'

'Daddy went to Delhi often on business and Mummy was able to accompany him on occasions, but the children never joined them on those trips. They were working trips.'

'Your Daddy was always in demand, poor man, always on the go. Your parents were such good people. They paid my tuition fees to become a nurse, they also paid for some of my sisters to go to college. I always think of them with great admiration.'

'Thanks for your kind words, Diana. They were good parents. And had never mentioned educating others. I appreciate you telling me.'

I reflect on how my parents, not far away from their retirement years, had sacrificed a very comfortable Indian lifestyle when they decided to take us children to Australia and begin over.

Diana acknowledges my comments with a nod as she pours tea and serves porridge. She moves in a rush between the kitchen and dining room, bringing freshly made dhal puris, lentil puffs and sauces. Excusing herself, she looks through the glass pane on her front door before returning to her kitchen.

Now, I have goosebumps thinking about the day that Hannah and I looked out of the glass pane of our front door. Sometimes, we had to look together, one eye each. There were ten, maybe more, men on our veranda. A few of them carried out something thin, long and lumpy, covered in a white cloth from under the stairwell. It took them a very long time to get it out. Finally, they laid it on a concocted platform on the veranda.

'Hannah, what do you think that is?'

'It's a body.'

'How do you know?'

'I can make out a head shape under the cloth.'

'OK, it's a body then, but whose?'

'Manju, I say.'

'It is not, I can see Manju.'

'He is not there.'

'Yes, he is. Look, he is standing near the body.'

'Is not.'

I didn't care what Hannah said. I could see him. Together, we watched, but saw different things. The men, with drooping jaws and eyes, wrung hands. They talked, but we couldn't hear what they said. Heads wobbled from side to side. We didn't know if they meant yes or no, good or bad. Other men carried buckets of water to the veranda. Our view was blocked by the men forming a human fence around the white cloth. Although we couldn't see clearly what was going on, we thought that they were washing whatever they had dragged out from under the stairwell. Hannah and I were complaining that they were taking forever. Just then, the men stepped back and we got a good look at what Hannah had previously said was a body, now wrapped in a crisp white cloth.

'They have shrouded the body,' said Hannah.

'What's that?' And I remembered that a few days ago she had mentioned something about when Jesus died. 'Is that the shroud of Turin?'

'Don't be so stupid. There is no face of Jesus on it!'

'Okay, I just wondered.'

The body was covered with yet another white cloth and tied at each end, in what looked like a sweet's wrapper.

'Look, Hannah, they made a bonbon.'

The men lifted the bonbon and placed it onto a *khatia*. The cheap wooden bed was then raised on timber posts. The men took up a position – one at each corner of the *khatia,* and two on either side. They folded their right hands over the left on their breasts. Another man, who we barely recognised and was possibly a priest or leader, stood at the head of the shrouded body. Although we did not understand what he said, it sounded like prayers, sacred and solemn. A few minutes later, in chorus, '*Assalaamu Alaikum.* God is great,' said the men. We had heard these words in their daily greetings to each other, the Alaikum anyway. Their recitation continued while four men hoisted the *khatia* off the posts onto their shoulders and carried it away.

We heard Mummy's voice and left our viewing post in a hurry, considering ourselves lucky that neither Mummy nor Nana had caught us or we would have missed the whole thing. We heard voices on the veranda chattering together in a chant – holy and harmonious. The intense cloying smell of incense burning crept under our doors, filling the rooms.

Hannah and I wasted no time in taking our dolls into the backyard. We filled containers with water and poured it over the dolls. With hand towels, we soon made our own bonbons with twisted ends.

Mummy walked past just as a whiff of phenyl pierced the air. She stopped. 'Thank goodness, it is over. They are disinfecting,' she said. She then looked at Hannah and me, and the bonbons. 'What are you doing?'

'Nothing, Mummy.' I crossed my legs.

'*Chullo*,' said Ayah, hauling us off to the bathroom.

Hannah didn't need to go, but neither of us wanted to talk to Mummy at this time.

On our way out of the bathroom, we walked past the drawing room, to find Mummy on her knees. She must have heard us and called for us to join her in prayers.

Stunned, Hannah and I looked at each other. This would cut into our playtime, but we knew there was no use in trying to get out of prayers. Like heavenly angels, we knelt under the picture of the Sacred Heart of Jesus. When everyone had gathered, Mummy held up the crucifix on her rosary, kissed it and made the sign of the cross. I bowed my head.

'Let us pray for the recently departed. Grant him peace, Lord.' Mummy kissed the crucifix again and continued, 'I believe in God, the Father Almighty…'

I nudged Hannah. 'What's departed?'

She shrugged. I will have to ask Mummy later, I thought.

I looked around at everyone in the room and noticed that Nana had strung her rosary beads over her small, white, bony fingers. She had neat darning on the sleeve of her blue cardigan. Hannah was fiddling with a hole in her shoe. Nelson was playing with pieces of Techno. Mary, Bible in hand, had her eyes firmly closed, while Catherine was looking through pattern books. I continued to scan the room until my eyes nearly fell out of their sockets. The box and chair that Hannah and I had used for our investigation was still at the front door. I wished I knew the words to pray. If I ever needed prayers, it was now. But I did not know the prayers as well as everyone else did. Yet. So, every time we had to say, 'Amen,' I said it in my loudest voice, and hoped that God had heard me.

Mummy had rolled her rosary beads all the way around to the start. Soon, prayers would be over. I closed my eyes, squeezed them tight, 'Amen, Amen, Amen,' I said. When I opened my eyes, Mummy was getting off her knees. Soon she would open her eyes. Hannah and I would need more than prayers to save us if Mummy found out that we had looked out of the windowpane. My tummy churned in fear.

Hannah knew the consequences too. She hopped on one leg. 'Ouch, ouch.'

'What's the matter, Hannah?' Mummy asked.

'My foot hurts,' she wailed.

'Come here, let me take a look.'

At that precise time, Alison began to whinge and Mummy rushed out of the drawing room, telling Hannah, 'Wait, I will be back to take a look.'

Hannah's foot made a miraculous recovery as soon as Mummy left the room. 'My foot feels better, Mummy. No need for you to come back.'

And now, for the very first time since Mummy brought Alison home, I loved that terrible whine. Hannah and I bolted to the front door. Speed was of the essence in dismantling our viewing contraption. Manju entered the drawing room, holding his broom.

'Manju, help us, please,' I said.

Hannah rolled her eyes at me. Manju didn't help, but Hannah and I were swift to get it all down before Mummy returned with Alison. We smiled like cherubs and offered to play with Alison.

Mummy put her down and thought it was time we all had refreshments. Ayah had prepared high tea and we sat together eating dainty, cucumber ribbon sandwiches and iced cakes.

Later that evening, we were given permission to go out onto the front veranda. Manju was sitting under the stairwell. Ghee-soaked wicks in clay pots replaced his belongings. I watched the flickering lights, and overheard the neighbourhood people saying, 'The sweeper boy expired from typhoid.' I understood the words sweeper boy.

At sunset, naturally I had to come indoors. Soon it was dinner time and I was cutting cutlets on my plate, when I thought it was the perfect time to ask, 'Mummy, early this morning, an old uncle with silver hair and round glasses talked to me. He knew all about my birthday party.'

I watched Mummy scrunch her serviette.

'Mummy, I have never seen the old man before. Where does he live?'

'He no longer lives here, he has gone,' she said and the colour drained from my mother's lips. Her eyebrows shot up to her forehead, she raised her hands, dropped her head into them. And the dining room became silent.

I thought I would fill in the void. 'Mummy, what does departed mean?'

Mummy bit her lower lip, dropped her hands down. 'Departed means gone for a very long time…forever.'

'Who was the departed that we prayed for today, Mummy?'

'Manju.'

'Mummy, Manju has not departed.'

'Yes, Gwen, sadly last night. And so has the old man you saw this morning, a long time ago.'

'No, Mummy, Manju was in the house after we prayed the rosary and he is still under the stairwell.'

My mother did not so much as look in my direction, 'Gwen, we will need to have a talk someday. I have a migraine, my head pounds. Excuse me.'

In my room at Diana's place, deep gratitude flows to my mother for protecting me as she did. I realise all the distress and concern I must have caused her with my innocent but terrifying queries.

Diana alerts me that my driver has arrived for my ride to the airport. Am I being disloyal to my mother, I wonder.

'I'll be there in a moment,' I call out.

I thank Diana, who has been the perfect hostess this morning, and depart, albeit not for long.

'*Salam*, ma'am,' the driver greets me.

'*Salam*. How are you today?'

'Ma'am, you don't have big luggage?'

'Not this time, driver.'

'Ma'am, we have plenty of time. You want to have little drive around the city while it is still very quiet?'

'No, thank you, I want to go straight to the airport.'

'Ma'am, I am getting you to the airport in plenty of time. Little trust for me, ma'am.'

I agree to a slight detour on the condition we are out of the city before peak time.

9

The sun spreads a fine saffron mist over the city. Worshippers scurry on foot to temples. Businesses make daily food offerings to deities; pedlars uncover night canvases from street stalls. Women with stiff-stick brooms sweep around homes to invite good fortune for the new day. Milk vendors, aluminium milk pails balanced on either side of bicycles, make their delivery rounds.

'Paper, paper!' An urchin boy's call catches my attention and I turn my head in the direction of the cry.

The Statesman House comes into view. In disbelief, I hold my hand to my mouth. It is my father's newspaper building and I had planned on visiting it on my return to Calcutta.

'Ma'am, this is one of the city's finest buildings.'

'Stop.' I intend for the driver to stop talking so as to relish the moment. Instead, he stops the car. I am directly outside the building.

The gatekeeper has unlocked the red iron gates and, childlike, I bolt to the building's entrance, stopping at the revolving door. And I am taken back to the many times I had been here as a child. During school holidays, Nelson, Hannah and I accompanied Aladdin, the family's driver, to fetch Daddy from work; we parked in the driveway.

The odour of printer's ink wafts into my nostrils. I could almost taste it on my tongue, tangy, thick. It travels into my eyes, making them smart, the same way it did all those years past. A peon, carrying numerous bundles of paper tied with strings of various colours, hesitates at the revolving door. It reminds me of how I usually hesitated at that door, particularly on the day that it was my turn to run to Daddy's office and alert him to his ride home.

That day, management had been taken hostage. Mr Banerjee, babu, clerical worker, didn't give his usual laugh or say, 'Scared again, Gwen? Don't be. When you come to an opening, just walk out.' As he did on the occasion when he helped me find my way out. 'Your father is not in his office,' he said reservedly, and returned to his desk.

'Where is he, Mr Banerjee?'

'Maybe you do not wait today.' His voice trembled while he massaged his forehead. In his white dhoti and kurta, he looked stiff, almost as if he had been dropped fully clothed into a vat of starch.

Past the grand foyer I strode toward the stairs leading to my father's office. Women in colourful gold-bordered saris wrapped tightly around them showed off midriff. They looked smart with their black hair infused with coconut oil, pulled back in buns or plaits. It was usual for the workers to acknowledge my presence with a small wave. Instead, that day, they made what appeared to be unnecessary adjustments to already tidy piles on their desks.

It was the first time that I had been in Daddy's office alone. It gave me time to look at his framed awards, certificates and photographs of him the day he met Mahatma Gandhi, along with a framed copy of the front page of the 30 January 1948 edition of the Mahatma's assassination. Also a photo of him, Sir Edmund Hillary and Tensing Norgay, the Nepalese-Tibetan sherpa who accompanied Sir Edmund, on their return from the summit of their Mount Everest expedition in 1953. There were photographs of other people and events too, which must have been important to Daddy.

Copies of previous issues of the newspaper were on his desk, but it was odd that the next day's newspaper wasn't there, ready to be reviewed, when it should have been. There was no clack-clack, clack-clack from the printing presses. The lithograph machine and typesetting plates were unused. In the corner, the refrigerator hummed louder with no competition from the sound of other machines. Although the cups from the silver tea service on a sideboard did not require rearranging, I tidied them and with my finger, wrote my initials on a frosty jug, with remnant pieces of ice floating on top.

I settled into Daddy's high-backed chair and felt as if I were sinking into a cloud. Now that I was in charge at his big desk, orders were issued to pretend employees. Through the magnifying glass, I inspected newsprint closely and circled the errors in red.

Where was my father? I stuck my face to the glass pane which overlooked the entire printing floor. A handful of workers were talking beside the machines. My breath fogged the glass. I wiped it with my sleeve, gazed up and down the long concrete aisles, noticing that printing machines and folding machines with paper loaded on them remained silent. Occasionally, someone glanced up in my direction and I waved. In turn they shifted and looked away.

Daddy always wore a suit, shirt and tie to work. That made it easy to spot him on the machinery floor. His milky-white skin stood him apart from most others who had rich dark skin, and wore white lungis, shirts and caps.

There was a knock on the office door.

'Come in.' I put on my best important-sounding voice.

The handle turned and Mr Banerjee entered. 'Please, Gwen, you must go home.'

'I am not going without my father. He has to come home.'

'Sahib has to stay here tonight.'

'Why? Where is he?'

'Please, you must go home. Come, come…'

He escorted me to the revolving door. By now, the entire ground floor administrative staff had left for the day. Two men with chains and padlocks waited at the gate. I got into the car.

'Daddy is not in his office, Mr Banerjee said we had to go home without him,' I told Nelson and Hannah.

'What's happened to Daddy?' Hannah scowled, but Nelson was excited at the news.

'Mr Banerjee did not say.'

The men with chains motioned to us to leave. We left through the gate, and they were quick to close and fasten the chains.

When we were some distance from Daddy's office, Driver stopped the car. He and Nelson swapped seats.

'What are you doing, Nelson?' said Hannah.

'Taking a driving lesson.'

At fourteen, driving came naturally to Nelson, and it was apparent from the ease in which he handled the switchover into the driver's seat that he had done this before. Hannah and I were unconcerned about him driving.

It was dusk. The street lights glowed orange as we zigzagged through a junction. Following cars, we dodged vegetable carts being wheeled down the street and diverted around a cow and her calf. At every intersection, there was a rusty oil drum with a policeman standing on it, directing traffic. Hannah and I were still talking about Daddy when, with a thump-thump, we were thrown forward in an abrupt stop.

At the intersection, a policeman was swaying on his drum, arms flailing, legs spanned as if he were on a rough sea. The drum moved in a small circle, creating sounds like small claps of thunder as it slowed and came to a halt. The policeman pointed his lathi at our car, brandishing the two-foot-long rounded stick frantically. He looked down, possibly for his wooden crate steps, but they were gone. In an instant, a mob had encircled the crime scene.

Aladdin was quick to jump out of the car. 'Children, keep the windows and doors shut,' he ordered us.

The policeman unceasingly wielded the lathi at him. Aladdin casually reached into his back pocket. From it, he took out his wallet, pulled some money out of it and handed it up to the policeman. With a scowl, the policeman inspected the money and pursed his lips. He shook a finger at Aladdin, who again opened his wallet and handed him more money, and then shook his open wallet vigorously. The policeman slipped the offerings into his back pocket and waved us on. The mob shrugged and parted. We drove off. Case closed.

On reaching home, Mummy was concerned as to why we were so late, and without Daddy. I told her that Mr Banerjee said that Daddy had to stay.

'Did you see other people in the building? What about Mr Menas, Mr Gomes or Mr Mohammed Ali?' Mummy picked up the phone. After a few minutes, she said, 'It rang out,' and replaced the receiver softly in its cradle. 'Tell me everything that happened in the office.'

I sat and gave Mummy every detail about what Mr Banerjee had said and some of what I did in Daddy's office in his absence.

The phone rang.

'Hello.' Mummy cupped the receiver with her hand. 'It is Mr Banerjee,' she whispered. 'Yes, Gwen told me that, but can you not tell me now why sahib could not come home?' She listened for some time, 'How can you be so sure that he is safe?' She remained silent for a while. 'Okay, I will not ring again or tell anyone that you have contacted me, Mr Banerjee. I will wait for your call.' Mummy hung up the receiver, bit on her lower lip, then said, 'My instinct tells me to do nothing. That way, I will not make matters worse for him and everyone else.' She must have meant the other people who might also still be in the office.

Mr Banerjee called the next day to let us know that Daddy was okay. News on the radio reported that in the locality of Daddy's office police had opened fire on protesters and resorted to tear gas. Bonfires were lit outside his office building, fuelled by newspapers. Threats were being made against management. Amongst those threats, murder was alleged.

Despite the daily calls from Mr Banerjee, uncertain as to what was happening in the office building, the family were very concerned for our father's safety. Authorities had been shut out and access made impossible without endangering those who were within.

After three tense days, early one morning, Daddy returned home with bloodshot eyes and in crumpled clothes. Mummy rushed to get him a drink of tea. He said that he needed more than a cup of tea but wanted a bath first. For now, he needed rest. Although relieved to see him and anxious to find out what had happened in the office, the family had to go about their usual activities for the day.

On our return from school and work, Mummy filled us in on the details at dinner. 'The industrial strike was called because workers wanted more pay and improved conditions. Management were taken as hostages and held in a room until the union considered that a favourable decision had been reached.'

It was a surprise to hear that Daddy had been locked in the same area as all the other executives; usually, the workers were nice to him. During Indian festivals, Daddy's employees sent him big circular hampers. Nelson, Hannah and I would sit on our haunches around them and inspect their contents through cellophane – six-inch hollow-centred multicoloured sweets moulded from pure sugar and shaped in the likeness of deities or obelisks; or other sweets, dependent on the festival. Included were spinning tops, dolls, cricket sets and skipping ropes and our favourite food delicacies of tinned guava cheese, famous Amul butter, Bandle cheese, gooseberry jam, plump red lychees and ripe mangoes with an aroma that tantalised and tempted us to break open the hampers.

Mary used to warn us that Daddy would send them back. We didn't like her suggestion and tried ignoring her. Alas, when Daddy got home, we watched with resentment as he returned all the goodies to their respective senders with cards, 'Humble thanks and gratitude.'

Daddy viewed all these gifts as bribes or unnecessary because the families who had sent them were more in need of the items than he.

'The strikers could not let him go, because the men had told him that their actions would not be taken seriously if they spared him. Besides, he was the one person in management who they could rely on to reach a sensible agreement,' said Mummy.

At dinner, Daddy told us it had not been so bad for him during the lock-up. Workers had looked after him with food and drinks. Also, they brought him toiletries, and a fresh towel, so he could freshen up each morning. The remainder of the executives were only offered water and snacks and given regular chairs with straight backs or wooden seats. When the hostages needed to use the lavatory, the strikers waited directly outside the door and hurried them along. Although Daddy had told them he refused to be treated differently to his colleagues, each night he was escorted to his office, where he slept in his recliner chair. On reaching an agreement, Daddy was the first to be released and the workers apologised to him for all the inconvenience they had caused him over the last few days.

Of course, Daddy always protected us from the reality of what he faced regularly, but we were happy with his report and listened without blinking until he said, 'I noticed a dent in the front bumper bar of the Dodge.'

Hannah, Nelson and I made a quick exit.

'Ma'am, can we go?' the driver pleads with me at the revolving door.

'I am sorry, driver. I did not intend to hold us up.'

I settle back in the car and my mind shifts back to the many times my father had been through industrial strikes; each time, management was threatened with bodily harm. I now make sense of the full impact of what he must have faced in his position time and time again. He was held responsible for all printed copy, regardless of whether he was at his desk or not. My poor father, despite all, never let family share that burden. It is at this moment that I appreciate the fear he must have held for our family on the day we escaped from the country. Some of that anxiety begins to run through my veins. I wonder why had the driver singled out the Statesman House building to show me this morning. I had not mentioned my father to him; it is not en route to the airport from where we began the journey. Had authorities on my arrival connected me with my father? Could they do anything to me? I remain silent for the rest of the trip, allowing my insecurities to play out in my head.

As soon as we arrive at the airport, I jump out of the car. 'Thank you, driver.' I hand him payment together with a tip and tell him he need not get out himself.

His face is a series of contortions with my behaviour, but I assure him that I am fine.

'*Salam*, ma'am.' He bids me farewell.

I walk briskly, mechanically getting my ticket out of my handbag to show the security guard at the entrance.

'Not this section, ma'am. You need domestic.'

I hesitate for a moment and then ring the driver. 'You've dropped me at the wrong terminal. Come back and take me to the correct one.'

'Sorry, ma'am, can't do that, not my jurisdiction. I will ring my friend there and he will take you.'

My blood pressure is rising, but I have no choice. Twenty minutes passes before another car arrives. The ride is less than five minutes. Had I known that, perhaps I could have walked. When satisfied that I am at the correct place, I pay the driver and proceed to my flight, which is due to depart within the next half hour. The extra time that I had allowed myself has dissipated and I rush to the departure gate, expecting to be the last person to board, but there is no one at the gate. Passengers are strewn all over the terminal. Perhaps there were announcements which I have missed.

I find a few passengers due out on the same flight as me, but they are none the wiser. They appear unconcerned; perhaps to them, this is a common occurrence. They are milder-mannered than me and when I suggest we get an answer, they look at me and raise their shoulders as if I am talking gibberish.

At the departures counter, I wait my turn for what seems an eternity but is probably two minutes. Ignored, I knock on the counter, 'Excuse me,' I call, in a controlled and friendly tone.

It's useless being agitated. Indians nod and smile sweetly, whether you are beating up on them or being courteous – it's all the same.

'You have to wait,' a perky voice responds.

With strained patience, I wait an unbearable fifteen minutes and repeat the knock.

'You have to wait.'

I will not wait any longer. I show a little of my Western impatience, where everything must happen immediately. 'When is the delayed flight to Chennai departing?'

'That is not my job to know. The person in charge of that information is not here.'

'Who is that person? Where are they? And when do you expect them back?'

'Some information is coming soon, ma'am.'

That information did not come for twenty-four hours. I was furious and my constant chasing up did nothing other than irritate me.

On the last occasion of my visit to the departures counter, I throw my hands in the air. 'Bloody Indian bureaucracy,' I murmur – and spend my night on a seat in the departure lounge.

10

It is late afternoon of the next day when I arrive in Chennai, formerly colonial Madras, on the Coromandel Coast, Bay of Bengal, Eastern India. Home to Fort St George, once the roots of the British military garrison and the East India Company trading post, as well as some of my family's roots.

Perspiration rolls down my head and face. I want to shelter indoors from the sultry heat but I do not have any more time to waste. I hail a tuk-tuk, a three-wheeler motorised vehicle with a yellow cabin and black soft-top roof.

In Chennai, I am at a total loss for the local language. India has hundreds of dialects spread across its various states. English is universal, so I get by. From my numerous trips to this city as a child to visit my mother's relatives, I am able to recall the street address of my aunt's house in which we stayed while holidaying in Madras. I ask the driver to take me there.

Filled with confidence, the tuk-tuk driver weaves through traffic congestion. After fifteen minutes he calls out, 'Which way, ma'am?'

My memory fails me with the details to recognise the place, and there have been many changes over the decades since I was last here.

'Why didn't you say you didn't know how to get there?' I asked.

'Don't worry, ma'am, it will only cost you little more fare. Ma'am, I need some petrol.'

I want to scream but control myself.

He stops the tuk-tuk, pulls a can from the back someplace and informs me he will be back soon and, 'Ma'am, I need some petrol money.'

Exasperated, I give him a couple of hundred rupees, eight Australian dollars. He returns within a few minutes and then chit-chats with other drivers along the way, which I consider is about how he should get me to my destination. He takes me down a street and a glimpse of memory returns.

'Left turn here, driver,' but to my disappointment the entire area has been industrialised and there is nothing familiar. My heart sinks but I close my eyes, put on a brave front and relish the memory of many fun holidays here. 'Driver, can you take me to the nearest Catholic church?'

Within a few minutes, and by sheer luck is my hunch, we are outside a cream building with a brown painted outline that resembles a hexagon, crowned with a crucifix. Below it, encased in glass, the figure of the Virgin Mother.

Once-familiar English signage has been replaced with a south Indian language that I don't know. I take off my shoes, place them alongside dozens of others at the entrance and step inside the church. The pews have been removed and the floor is covered in coir mats. People are sitting on them cross-legged. At the altar, I light candles in memory of my parents, who had been married here, cousins who would have received sacraments and the many times during visits to Madras that I had been in here.

Although I cannot recall the exact location or even the layout of the church buildings, I search for the vestry. As the family historian, I must collect certificates for the family tree being collated.

Outdoors is a slender young man with thick tight curls as dark as coal. He is wearing sandals and a white robe and holding a Bible.

I race over to him, 'Excuse me, Father. I am looking for the administration building.'

'Please, come this way. I am Father Thivan, the parish priest. How can I help you?' His English is thick with a Tamil accent. 'If you require information, it cannot be done today. It is a feast day and we are busy. Can you come back tomorrow morning?'

Although I would have preferred if he could have done it today, I am left with no choice. I thank the young priest and leave, confirming my return the next day.

Outside, my tuk-tuk driver is playing cricket with a plastic ball in a laneway, amongst local children. He hastens back to me and enquires as to my visit. I tell him that I need to return tomorrow and he is all smiles.

'You like to eat some nice south Indian food, ma'am.'

'A grape juice would be nice.'

Driver draws a long smile and takes me to what is known as the world's second longest urban beach. I had spent considerable time here as a child during holidays with cousins in the south of India at Marina Beach. Fort St George extends from the north, for thirteen kilometres, with six of them being promenade. The heat draws people to this sandy beach, where they bathe in the water fully clothed. Food stalls, a merry-go-round, pony rides, picnics, cricket and fortune-tellers are set up on the sand.

I stroll along the statue-filled seafront, grape juice in hand. At the statue of Annie Besant, I hear my father's voice recounting the British socialist, women's rights activist, prolific writer…and champion of human freedom. I am inspired with that thought.

My interest in yoga brings me to stop at the statue of an Indian monk, Swami Vivekananda a nineteenth-century disciple of Indian mystic Ramakrishna who introduced Indian philosophies and yoga to the Western world. A shiver steals down my spine.

I must organise a place for my stay. While sipping on my grape juice, I catch sight of a hotel overlooking the water. I ask my driver to take me there. I decide to stick with this driver. In addition to the fare, I had filled his tank. Why risk a new driver who would certainly have me go through it all again?

From my hotel balcony at dusk, I watch thousands of people cram the beach, with no lifeguards in sight. I too feel as if I am swimming without a lifeguard. In my notebook, I scribble names and dates for my visit to the church administration the next day.

At breakfast, I sample south Indian food. I had long forgotten the taste of idly and sambar, fluffy, steamed, fermented rice cakes with spicy gravy. Although not a coffee drinker, I find the percolating smell of strong black coffee irresistible.

The driver drops me on the street as near to the church administration office as possible. The door is shut. I consider the priest is running late and spend the time watching a constant stream of devotees flock into the church across from it, a throng of people surrounds a temple. It makes me wonder, why are Indians so devout?

Half an hour passes. Frustrated with the time that I have already waited, I decide to leave and make my way down the church steps.

A young man in a Western shirt and pants, wearing rubber slippers, races up to me. 'Father will be here soon,' I'm told.

I had already understood that 'soon' in India and time do not equate. And laugh.

The young man opens the office door and gives me a toothy smile. 'You can wait inside.'

The white-walled administration room is long and narrow, with numerous rows of timber shelves, each holding bound folios. Ceiling fans click the heat away. A mound of religious medals, prayer books and holy pictures are on display for sale. I am reviewing my short list of names, when the door opens. Father Thivan's wiry hair is tamed. I smell coconut oil. His prominent lips are shadowed by thick, black spectacle frames.

'Sorry, I had to administer last rites to an elderly parishioner.'

Time is of the essence for me, though thankfully not in the same way. The heat is consuming and I feel if he doesn't hurry, I may be in need of last rites myself.

'We cannot predict the time the Lord beckons us to him, Father. No problem keeping me waiting.' I lie in a holy place.

Although late, the priest is in no rush to assist me and begins a task at his desk. I twiddle my thumbs.

A quarter of an hour passes before he looks at me. 'What would you like me to find?'

'Thank you. I'd like copies of a couple of certificates, please.' I hand him my list with names and the exact date of my parents' marriage and for the baptism, an approximate date. I know that Catholics usually christen babies as soon after birth as possible.

Father Thivan studies the list of two, as if they are some extensive demands, then cleans his glasses and gets a stepladder. By now, I know that impatient people cannot survive in India. Through my own experiences, I have already learned that Indians have a time clock of their own – whatever time they make it.

'I used to visit this church when we holidayed in Madras.'

'Imagine that.' He wanders off.

From an upper shelf, Father extracts a large folio, braces its weight against his chest. I stand up to assist but am waved off as he places it on the table. He opens it to April 1941, flips through pages. When satisfied, he swivels the book to face me, and returns to the paper that I had handed him. I scroll my eyes down the page of marriages solemnised. On a single line, of the day on which my parents' married, I see handwritten signatures of my parents and the witnesses to their marriage – my paternal grandfather and another name, unknown to me. In a flash, I recall my mother's favourite story, told to me many times as a child and again as an adult.

11

From Mummy's lips, plump, ripe as recently-picked berries, came another tale. 'Did I tell you about your father's and my wedding? I was young – seventeen years old. I had been out of school for two years and worked as a typist at the railway. One Sunday afternoon, in March of 1941, I had just finished a piece of fine needlework for a client of my Auntie Amy and joined my brothers Clarence and Ernest, my sister Merlyn and her husband, John, who were practising violin, ukulele and guitar for a show that we were to perform the following week. I was playing the guitar when your father's parents unexpectedly visited our home. Well, it was unexpected to me anyway.' Mummy twirled her wedding band around her finger. 'They had come to ask for my hand in marriage. Your father wasn't even with them. I had seen him only a very few times before, and I knew that he had dashing good looks, but we had not spoken often. My father died when I was nine years old – conjured.'

'What do you mean?'

'An evil spell was cast on him.'

'How did you know that?'

'Everyone did. He had unexplained pain that couldn't be diagnosed medically.'

'Could it mean that back then they couldn't identify disease, medical problems, as they can today?'

'No.'

'Tell me more about this. What kind of pain did he have? And where…?'

'I don't want to discuss that now, Gwen. We are talking about marriage, not death. They asked my mother, Mabel, for my hand in marriage. She in turn had to ask permission from my eldest brother, Clarence. After much thought and scrutiny, he agreed to the proposal. I was given a say in the matter, but by and large it was their decision.' Mummy continued twirling her wedding band.

'Why did she have to ask Uncle Clarence?'

'That's how it was – the tradition. You ask too many questions, Gwen. Just listen! The next day, my mother and brother received an official letter to mark the discussion of the previous day. As per the custom of our community in Madras at that time, the same letter was returned on a silver tray, lined with a white doily and red roses. If the response was 'no', we would have been required to return the same letter without the tray.

'The following week, the parish priest was contacted to attend the formalities. Family and friends were invited to witness him bless the engagement ring and your father place it on my finger. Your grandpa, Herbert, chose it – a thick gold band with "SAM", short for Samuel, in solid gold lettering on top.' My mother held up the ring as if she were now Lord of the Ring.

'Following our engagement, your father was permitted to visit me each evening, but we never went out unchaperoned, except on one occasion, to the pictures.

'The wedding was arranged within weeks for the end of April 1941. The venue chosen by your grandpa was Government House, Madras. He had been Governor Willingdon's personal bodyguard for a considerable time and also a member of the government band.

'It was during World War II and the lavish marquees that were erected to take full use of the gardens had to be camouflaged. The entire reception area was covered with exquisite pink and white roses. The wedding sofa and arch above it swathed in a similar theme. Nana's brother, John, was in charge of the gardens in Government House. He ordered all the roses from the rose gardens at Ootacamund in the Nilgri Hills, around five hundred kilometress away from Madras.

'At five-thirty on a spring evening, at North George Town, Assumption Church, Madras, we were married. The hour-and-a-half-long ceremony was presided over by Father Antos, accompanied by organist and singers. It was terrifying, but I went along with it all.'

'Did your Auntie Amy make your wedding gown?'

'Yes, a full-length gown, made from white silk, embellished with silver star-shaped cachous, all embroidered by hand. It was soft and comfortable. My headpiece, a ring of white roses, held up a long train that flowed down, and my bouquet of red roses, a special gift from John M., also came from the Ootacamund Hills.' She paused. 'They were so fragrant. Coral Hurley, a friend of mine, was my bridesmaid, and the three flower girls were Rita Mitchell and her sister, whose name I don't remember now.' She raised her eyebrows. 'I don't know why they had to be flower girls. Anyway, Myrtle, your father's sister, who was about nine or ten years old, also attended me.

'Following the ceremony, back in Government House, guests welcomed us under a giant confetti bell, supplied by the governor. Freddie Jones, the best man, who your father barely even knew and was soon to wed Coral, broke the bell. Confetti fluttered in all directions. The governor's band played the grand march, while we circled the cake three times before cutting it. My attendants then distributed fingers of cake on silver trays. Refreshments preceded a sit-down dinner at eight-thirty. Fine silverware, crystal, luxurious linen, silver serviette holders, candelabras and enough waiting staff that you did not need to lift a finger to help yourself with anything, it can only be described as a Grand Affair.

'It was almost two o'clock the next morning when we had the final wedding waltz. I went home with my mother. Your father went home with his parents. We were compelled to attend a blessing Mass together at seven the next morning, after which we were required to visit the homes of various relatives as husband and wife. Then, together we went to live with Nana and Grandpa.' She lingered a moment and her perky lips disappeared.

'In 1942, the war still raged. Fighter planes flew over Madras. Towards the end of that year, I gave birth to Patricia. It was only days after

I had left the hospital when a bomb, intended for the Madras Fort, was misjudged and the general hospital was partially destroyed instead.'

Shuddering, she continued, 'Air raid sirens blared. Your father hurried us into a trench and rushed away. As a volunteer air raid personnel (ARP) member, he was responsible to raise the alert and ensure that everyone in his care was in the trenches.'

Stopping as if it was all too much to handle, Mummy stared into space. 'I felt so alone.'

Alone in India! Physically seeing my parent's handwriting gives me comfort. I feel them surrounding me. Father Thivan transcribes the information onto ready-made forms and authenticates them. I leave the church on a high.

Travelling further south from Chennai into the coolness of the Western Ghats of the mountains, known as the Nilgri Hills lies nineteenth-century Ootacamund, considered to be the queen of the many hill stations the British created in India as their summer resorts. Originally the resting place for convalescing soldiers, it soon became home away from home for the British. The steam railway line, still in working order, is one reminder from that era. A stone house is the first bungalow built on the land that the British had bought from the local Toda, indigenous people. Its architecture boasts from its colonial days. At Elk Hill, the fragrance and beauty of the manicured rose gardens is overpowering and I smile while reminiscing the story of my mother's bridal bouquet – roses.

St Stephen's Anglican Church, an icon with its stained-glass windows and paintings, built in 1829 exclusively for the British, is where my paternal grandparents were married. Today, there is no one at the church to assist me with records. I am forced to leave a written request for them and hope they will forward me the certificates I seek.

Later in the day, I am fortunate enough to stumble upon what I believe to be a former National Parks and Wildlife employee. He agrees to take me through Mudumalai Wildlife Sanctuary. I am thrilled! My father had told me about this sanctuary that he had visited. It is almost three o'clock when the new-found guide takes me by open-air jeep down a dirt road, telling me that the sanctuary was home to about forty-eight tigers.

On the side of the dirt road there is a flurry of peacocks with tails fully spread, giving a dazzling display. Grey jungle fowls are darting around. After an hour or so in the sanctuary, there is a deep booming from the large brown deer, sambar.

'Ma'am, if sambar is calling, a tiger is nearby.'

Within minutes, the sanctuary erupts into a cacophony with an abundance of smaller spotted deer running for life. I hear the thud of big paws followed by a *brrr* and chuffing sound. Its distinct scent grows closer, and I see a tiger down at a watering hole.

I feel content with these experiences, and the time I have spent at the sanctuary. 'I'm okay to leave now, guide.'

'We can stay little longer, ma'am.'

We stay another hour driving around, when the guide informs me that he has lost his way out. It won't be long before we lose daylight and my knees begin to knock. I recall my mother's ominous reminder, 'In before dark.' In the distance, animal eyes shine.

The guide reassures me, 'They are only bison, ma'am, and don't usually charge the vehicle.' He casually continues, 'Once, ma'am, when I got lost, I encountered two tigers. That time, ma'am, I got a fine from the sanctuary for overstaying, but tigers never chase me.'

Unsure of what to make of this remark, I am fearful and uncomfortable with the fast-fading light around us.

'Ma'am, don't worry, the rangers will find and help us out.'

Despite my fears, I feel a sense of enormous joy. And amidst these two conflicting emotions, I realise that there is a slow simmering fire – a burning love of India. And headlights approach.

The next morning, I fly out to a major Hindu pilgrimage site, Varanasi, India's oldest and holiest city that lies on the banks of the sacred Ganges River.

12

My flight to Varanasi is not without incident and I arrive fashionably late in accordance with Indian time. It is dusk; the city is bathed in a haze of orange lights. The heady scents of sandalwood lace the electric air. Energy and excitement wrap around me and, as if in benediction, I engage in the thrum of this intoxicating city, where birth and death dominate daily rituals. Cymbals clash, drums beat and bells ring, warding off evil spirits. A scurry of twenty thousand or more people make their way to the liveliest part of the city, the ghats – wide stone steps that descend steeply into India's holiest River Ganges, for Arti – a Hindu offering fire ceremony.

I hasten out of the car, and a porter takes the luggage. I rush to meet Prakesh, my Indian guide for this evening.

A slender man with dark skin, in his early twenties, is pacing the hotel foyer, slicing his fingers through his thick dark hair, making it stand to attention. He catches sight of me and rushes over, his body bending in an exaggerated way from side to side, plasticine being remoulded with each step. 'Mrs Gwen?'

'Prakesh? Sorry, the flight out was delayed.'

'Hurry, ma'am, we don't want to miss the start.'

My running shoes do not complement my shimmering pink salwar with tiny mirrors sewn in, but they are practical. I drape my purple woollen shawl over my head and shoulders. We sprint from the hotel through a labyrinth of lanes throbbing with shelters selling betel nut, paan, food, drink, religious artiefacts, flowers and art. Dodging bulls, chickens, dogs, dung, pools of stagnant water and cows in the middle of the street, we make our way to the riverbank piled high with temples, palaces, pavilions and terraces.

I stop briefly to admire all that lies in front of me, and Prakesh's voice rises above the din.

'Come, ma'am, I have secured you a very good seat for the ceremony.'

'Thank you.'

I move as fast as I can until we reach a ceremonial marquee and find my front row, reserved seat. My very good seat is white plastic and dusty, the same as the other hundred or so here. Before I sit, the attendant rushes over, wipes the seat with a rag and offers me a bottle of water.

'Ma'am, give little money to the man for the good seat, the gods will smile on you,' says Prakesh.

I had already paid in advance for this good seat but, not wanting to miss out on a smile from the gods, I hand over a bundle of rupees to the attendant. From the joyous look on the attendant's face, I imagine the gods should smile on me a couple of times. I check the bottle's seal, take comfort that it is unbroken, also check that the bottom of the bottle has not been tampered with, refilled and patched – a god is smiling on me already.

Cymbals clash louder and bells ring, taking on a shimmy chime. Bhajans, holy songs, together with the beat of drums, climax in a single unified rhythm. Ceremonial silver sanctified lamps with several tiers and dozens of lighted wicks are carried through the crowds. Worshippers with extended hands reach towards the lamp, pass fingers over the flames, and touch their foreheads in devotion. Devotees repeat the words, bom bom bholey, or execute the hudukkar, the snorting of a bull by touching the tongue to the palate.

To announce the ceremony open, seven pandits blow into conch shells and welcome the goddess of the night. Clockwise, auspicious articles – flowers, incense and lighted lamps with wicks soaked in ghee – are held high above their heads, offerings to deities. At the same time, small handbells chime to chase away evil spirits. A pause to meditate.

Fifteen minutes or so passes, after which holy men weave through the hundreds of devotees and spectators, handing out marigolds and sprinkling holy water. Sadhus, robed in orange, schmooze through crowds, garlanding would-be disciples with roses and jasmine, hopeful for alms in return. Many followers, with eyes closed, look as if they have sunk into a deep meditative state. The atmosphere oozes with solemn piety.

Soaking up the ambience, wrapped in communal warmth, I close my eyes to hold the vibe under my lids, and a story related by my father comes to me.

On the outskirts of Calcutta, Daddy was surveying a parcel of land to purchase when he was targeted by a pickpocket. That morning, preferring not to draw attention from the local people by arriving in a private car, Daddy had travelled to the area by bus. On his way home, without money, he returned on foot. Being athletic, he was extremely fit and not deterred by the extensive distance that he estimated would take him four hours. The sun sweltered and the parched earth spread before him like a layer of heat-affected chocolate.

On his way, he thought about how to best develop the land, to benefit the locals. Soon, he realised that he had probably walked a quarter of the distance, when a sadhu appeared in front of him like an apparition. The holy man had his entire possessions at the end of a stick that he held over a shoulder with one hand. In the other, he swung an aluminium water canister.

'I never meet anyone while I walk this path, sahib. Where is it you are travelling on your journey?' said the sadhu.

'Calcutta.'

'That is a very long way from here, sahib.'

My father explained his situation. 'I feel sorry for the robber. He must have needed the money.'

'That is very fine philosophy, sahib. Please, can you hold out your palm?'

India and palm reading are synonymous. Daddy thought nothing of it and did as he was asked. The holy man laid down his belongings and held a fist over the exposed palm. He squeezed his fingers and a couple of milk drops trickled from the sadhu's compressed clutch into the lines and mounds of Daddy's palm below.

'Your life will always be blessed in abundance, sahib.'

Daddy held the milk, thick and snug in his grip. It tingled and glowed silver. The sadhu took his leave and vanished as quickly as he had materialised.

Within the next half kilometre, a car slowed beside Daddy. It was a fellow colleague.

'What are you doing walking alone in this remote place, sir?'

'Personal business.'

'I, myself, rarely come to this place. But yesterday, my mother's eldest brother's wife's first cousin…baby. Are you okay, sir?'

'Yes, thank you. Quite.'

'Come in the car, sir. I will take you home again.'

Since that day, Daddy claimed that he never knew want. All that was needed came. 'Be generous to those in need, no need to avenge your transgressors' was his message to family.

This memory makes me quiver. Glued to my seat, I sink into a place of deep veneration for my father. Chants and drums reverberate around me, reach a crescendo and stop. Conch shells sound and the ceremony concludes.

'Time to leave, ma'am,' says Prakesh and presents me with the bill for water.

I wonder, did I drink a whole crate of water and not realise it? I pay the bill, certain that it secures me a lifetime of smiles.

Early the next morning, I pull on a pair of jeans and a T-shirt, and wrap my best pashmina shawl around my shoulders. I walk down the ghat, to ride on a traditional rowing boat. The orange night streetlights are still aglow. An eerie fog clings high in the sky and low on the water of the Ganga, Ganges River. Small boats bob up and down in unison with the echo of pilgrims' prayers. The upper edge of the sun peeks through the horizon, the sky flames orange-reds, pink and yellow. Its reflection ripples in the water and cocoons me in this mystery.

At street level, at intermittent distances, numerous niches, roadside shrines, with lighted wicks in clay urns flicker. Hindu devotees swing clear plastic bags filled with oil, refill depleting urns. Following prayers, tilaka, a dot mark made from a paste – saffron for women and sandalwood for men – is placed at the centre of the forehead, as a symbol of the eye to the soul. Nearby, undisturbed on concrete floors, sadhus, beggars, monkeys and dogs sleep.

The boatman that I have chosen to ride with gives me a wide grin and garlands me with orange marigolds. The murky grey-green river water does not deter devotees. Men in lungi or trousers and women with rings in noses and hair decorated with white jasmine are immersed waist deep. Saris in hues of red, purple and green dot the water. The murmur of prayers ripples on the river.

In the rowboat, we glide along while pigeon flocks swoop, call and scavenge. Vendors plying up and down stream, peddle religious artefacts. Along the river, ablutions are performed, clothes washed. On the sandbanks, yoga is practised, dead bodies cremated, ashes cast into the river. A devout Hindu believes that in death, to be cremated and have your ashes dispersed in the Ganga will gain you moksha or release from the eternal cycle of rebirth.

At the conclusion of my ride, I sit on the bottom steps of the ghat to take in all that I have experienced and relish moments of equanimity.

A ten-year-old boy, in a cream kurta top, matching pyjamas and black rubber thongs, carrying a rattan basket on his left hip, approaches me. 'Ma'am, are you Indian?'

'I was born in India, but I'm Australian now.'

'Very good, ma'am. I am Amjeet. You want to go for boat ride? I can find you good boat.'

'No thank you, Amjeet. I've just returned from a boat ride.'

'Then buy a Patravali diya.' From his basket, he pulls a saucer-size container made from leaves. He shows me a candle with a ghee-soaked cotton wick at its centre, surrounded by marigolds. 'Five rupees for one, ma'am. If you make a wish and float a diya on the Ganga, God is smiling on you.'

I take a ten-rupee note from my pocket.

'Then two, ma'am.' The proficient salesman does not hesitate.

At the water's edge, my mini guide strikes a match, cups a hand around the wicks, hands me two lit diyas. With each one, he tells me to make a wish and release it into the Ganges River. Amjeet gazes at me with unwavering eyes, and his demeanour changes from that of a child to an old man.

'Ma'am, I am thinking the gods are liking you.'

I smirk. Didn't I pay for that privilege last evening? I look him straight in the eye, 'How do you know that, Amjeet?'

'Ma'am, your face is glowing.'

The river blurs before me.

'Many blessings to you and your family, ma'am.' The young wise man takes his leave.

I dry my eyes with my shawl, marvelling at the vibrancy of the ghats, a moving mosaic of colour and magnificence. Squatting at the water's edge, a woman in a blue chiffon sari, with green bangles on her arm, and a gold nose ring, has a child with a black string around its waist. Beside her there are two small earthenware pots. Untying a knot from the corner of her sari, she unfolds a neem stick and fills the pots with river water. From one of the pots, she pours water over the child's head, then her own. With the stick, she cleans her teeth, rinses, gargles and spits the water back into the river.

Curious, I wait a moment longer, when I am interrupted by a girl around eight years old. She is in a flimsy, knee-length Western dress. Her eyes are still filled with sleep and her hair is a tangled web.

'You are Australian, ma'am?'

'I am. News travels fast here.' I laugh. 'What's your name?'

'Nandi, ma'am.' She rubs her arms with vigour as if to warm them.

I remove my pashmina and wrap it around the child.

'The gods will smile on you, ma'am.' She pats my bare arms.

I laugh within, amused with all the smiles that I am getting from above.

'What are you selling?' I glance into the empty blue plastic wash dish held at her hip.

'Not much, ma'am, but I have twenty cents Australian – can you change it into rupees for me?'

'How much do you want for it?'

'What will you give me, ma'am?'

'Five rupees.'

Nandi's eyes flare open, bulge a little. She gasps for air. 'Noooooooo, the exchange rate is eight rupees for twenty cents – the dollar is worth forty rupees today.'

'Not the Australian dollar,' I say.

'Oh, yes ma'am, the Australian dollar was same as American dollar last week.'

Why should I, with my digital downloads, argue with a village girl? Astounded, I give her ten rupees, also her twenty cents back – so she could sell it to the next Aussie visitor.

'Can you buy some cookies for my little sister? She is hungry.'

At street level, from the local vendor, I buy two packets of cream crackers. Nandi puts the biscuits into her plastic dish, drapes the pashmina over them. We continue to walk another hundred metres when she fidgets with the pashmina and looks up at me.

'Ma'am, I have to go to school now.'

'Very well. I am happy to hear that you go to school. Where is your school?'

'Private school, ma'am. My car will come soon to pick me up. You want a lift somewhere, ma'am?'

I look to the heavens – certain the gods have stopped smiling and have broken into belly laughter.

From Varanasi, I venture south to Khajuraho. The smiley gods have surely accompanied me, because there is an occasional request from someone in a town or village through which I travel, eager to receive my blessing. I suspect it is because they want some of my smiley god fever to rub off on them.

The fact that I speak a certain level of Hindi, albeit in an Australian accent, precedes me at every place I visit along the way. Also, they know what I will buy and eat, and my age. They even know what my next destination will be and that I didn't collect my photographs taken kilometres away from where they are. Stumped, I wonder if perhaps they are a secret Indian mafia, arranged specifically for my visit.

My earthly driver and guide is protective and cautions me to watch my handbag. But no one tries to snatch it. On closer observation, nearly every Indian I meet has a 'cell', mobile phone. I don't feel threatened, so with each blessing request I oblige, and touch the top of a head or hand or else they touch my arm or my shawl. A broad smile or a head bobble says it all for me, they seem happy and I am too.

Khajuraho is a UNESCO World Heritage site and quiet village. At the hotel, eighteen lush acres of garden stretch before me. The air is fresh and the pool's azure water is inviting after a long day's journey. Coloured lights strung over a circle of trees in the garden illuminate paths and outdoor dining.

At the entrance foyer, rangoli, a decorative piece in Indian folk art pattern, created from coloured rice, grains, flower petals, dried flour and sand, occupies a third of the grand foyer's space. Thought to bring good luck, it is also used for festivals and to celebrate life's milestones.

Following a brief welcome and refreshments, I am taken by open-air jeep to view the monumental carved Hindu and Jain temples discovered four hundred years earlier. According to history, the eighty-five temples spread over six to nine square kilometres were built in a short span from AD 950 to 1050. But only twenty-two have survived the ravages of time.

It was believed that not long after their discovery, yogis and Hindus used them for annual pilgrimages. The Western Ghat or group of temples, being the most important of the three areas of temples, are said to be built on the theme of man and nature – Purusha and Prakriti, the source of life and creation.

Externally, the temples display rich and intricately carved statues with sexually explicit eroticism, and innumerable facets of Indian life are configured to express the central ideas of Hinduism – belief in a supreme being, and adherence to the concepts of truth, dharma (natural universal laws) and karma (deed, act, cause and effect). Inside, the walls are bare. Although not Hindu, I share these beliefs.

A local guide, Lucky, has been arranged to take me the following evening to the Western Ghat temples for a light and sound show.

Lucky arrives unusually early for a show that is not due to start for another few hours and I am not more than a ten-minute drive away from the venue. He jumps and skips along the path, laughing as if he is half crazed. It concerns me that he may be drunk, but his merriment settles down after a few minutes and he regains composure. We arrive at the venue earlier than the organisers. Lucky drops me off at the outdoor arena and runs off some place. A few minutes later, a young woman in a striking magenta and red sari sashays past me, heading in the same direction as Lucky.

A hundred white plastic chairs are set up, surrounded by stupendous sandstone creations. The monuments mimicking the ultimate fusion of man and his creator. Suspended in awe and reverence, I hold my breath and a gentle breeze through the trees creates a whisper. And something within unravels, my interconnectedness with India, the realms of life and the supernatural. Here, there is something infinitely bigger than me.

I turn to meditation. Later, with a clear mind, I contemplate on my yoga studies. In particular, Patanjali the codifier of yoga in his 195 sutras, divided into four padas, chapters, teaches that yoga is a path to inner freedom.

Samadhi pada is about thought and concentration, a blissful state of mind. Sadhana pada pertains to the instruction of the practice and discipline. Vibhuti pada is progression of the practice, the powers of yoga. It centres on the last three limbs of yoga – dharana, concentration; dhyana, meditation; and Samadhi, complete absorption which is the ultimate goal of yoga – a state of bliss and union with the spirit. The three limbs practised with the one object of thought is known as samyama. Through this, the benefits of extraordinary powers can result, which range from a physical level to the control of senses and sensations, ability to foresee the future and attain spiritual powers. And the dangers of falling under their spell.

Kaivalya pada is mastery of the mind, the goal of yoga – pure consciousness. In this division, the ways to attain powers and capabilities are shown. It explains how the mind is constructed, veils the inner light of the self and outlines five routes by which liberation or freedom can be attained. Of the five, yoga is one, and powers brought by birth another. Abilities received by the latter method are not considered the ideal way to acquire these skills, because it is thought if one has not followed the yoga path, one does not fully understand the route and risks misusing the supernatural powers or siddhis bestowed upon them.

As if a lightning bolt has struck me, electric currents run through my veins. My heart races, my hands tremble and my head spins. Was this a possible answer to my birth veil or why the spirit world contacted me long before I even knew they were spirits? A moment of deep, deep happiness comes over me and a resplendent blaze makes me feel humbled and ever so small. Feeling minuscule, I think about how desperately my mother had tried often for the correct timing to have a private talk with me, how resistant I had always been and how difficult it must have been for her to broach the subject.

In 1965, in the weeks leading up to my tenth birthday, my mother indicated that she wanted a talk with me. Skirmishes had again broken out with India and Pakistan over the disputed territory of Kashmir. India had opened up an international border near Sialkot, north-east

Pakistan, which escalated trouble and started the second Indo-Pakistan war since independence.

The border of East Pakistan, now known as Bangladesh, is close to Calcutta. Naturally, Calcutta was impacted by the warfare. Precautions had to be undertaken to darken window and door coverings to conceal any cracks of light that could be detected externally at night. Headlights were painted black at the top half to disperse light downwards and make it less conspicuous in the dark. Streetlights were also partially shaded. It was a time spent on a knife edge, listening to air raid sirens blaring with war planes flying overhead. By candlelight, we ate, talked and huddled around the radio, listening to reports of bombings in our city or elsewhere. Recalling reports that fighter pilot bombing raids were targeting hospitals still makes me want to retch.

The six months of horrors that year made Mummy forget about the proposed talk and I did not remind her, because chats always cut into playtime. I thought I had got away with it, but shortly before I would be a teenager, Mummy remembered and called me over to her.

Mummy sat on the sofa and I on the marble floor, hard but very cool on a hot summer's day. I knew that today's heart-to-heart wasn't about the birds and the bees. We never had those talks.

'These people you see,' said Mummy.

'Which people, Mummy?'

'Gwen, the ones you were never to tell the nuns or priests about.'

I shrugged. These instructions had been given to me since my first day at school when I was four and a half years old and have never stopped since.

'I don't know where to begin.' Mummy fidgeted with a magazine. 'I don't understand it but I know that it happens. If the nuns find out, they will probably make me keep you at home or, worse, report us to the bishop or send you to a doctor.'

'But I'm not sick.'

'No, not at all…but they appear to have chosen you of all my children.'

'Who has?'

'Your visitors.'

'Which visitors, Mummy?'

'Doctor Nag did warn me about something like this.' She swirled her hand in the air.

I didn't know exactly what Dr Nag had told my mother. Perhaps I should have paid more attention to Mummy when she spoke to me about these things. Not that Mummy would have given me the entire details anyway. My mother looked as if she had one of her big headaches coming on. I felt upset for her.

'Do you want an Aspro, Mummy?'

'No.' She wore her distance-gaze face.

Ayah asked if we wanted nimbu pani. Mummy's lips looked parched but she never responded.

I thought a fresh cold drink would be nice. 'Thanks, Ayah. Mummy and I would like that.'

Ayah left us with two tall glasses of the lemon drink with ice floating on top. Mummy did not touch her drink. I sipped mine, tasting the coolness.

'How are you enjoying the summer holidays, Gwen? Who have you seen since we moved into the new area?'

We had moved here a year earlier. I did not understand why my mother asked these unnecessary questions again.

'I love getting the tram to school. It feels grown up. The holidays were fun because we had lots of games lined up.'

I left out what we liked best – Mummy taking her afternoon nap. During that time, we filled water balloons and from the balcony dive-bombed them onto unsuspecting people passing by. Also, with the jointed legs and sharp points of a geometry divider, we pierced and hauled in fruit from vendor's baskets when they walked past the kitchen window.

Mummy's face had worry lines. I thought I was in for it. She had obviously found out what I especially didn't want her to know – that I had stayed in the crowd with servants to experience Chamali, our sweeper woman's daughter, give birth under a nearby stairwell. I had witnessed the blood-stained baby shown off by the proud grandmother, Lakshmi, singing '*Guryia, guryia, doll, doll,*' while its umbilical cord was still attached.

I panicked and wanted to leave. The budgerigars were chirping and I thought, if I distract Mummy by asking her about some of her favourite things, she might forget about Lakshmi.

'Mummy, have any of your budgies hatched as yet?' Knowing perfectly well they had not, because Mummy always got so excited with a new arrival that we all knew about it.

'They should start to hatch in a few more days.' And although we couldn't see the aviaries from where we were, Mummy looked in the direction of her small blue and green birds. In the cooler months, Mummy set up light bulbs over tiny light grey eggs to keep them warm. She also ensured a good supply of cuttlefish to keep up their calcium.

'Why don't you go and check them now, Mummy?' I stood up.

'Sit down, Gwen. I'll check them later.'

I sat. With a pale face, Mummy thumbed a corner of her *Woman's Weekly*, but I knew she did not realise that she was even doing it.

'The old man in striped pyjamas.'

'Which old man, Mummy? I have seen many.'

Mummy looked as if she was going to break and sighed deeply. 'Manju.' She rolled the magazine. 'They, they and so many others that you see.' Silence befell her momentarily and then she blurted, 'You, you see dead people and talk to them and them to you.'

My skin shrank. I know it did because it felt stiff around my bones. My chest tightened and I opened my eyes wide. Everything around me burst into commotion. The air was thick. Unbreathable.

'Don't be afraid, it is a gift,' I thought she said.

But the words were too late. Darkness flooded over me. The heat gave off what I thought was a potent mist. I lay still on the cold floor. My throat burned for a while, but then I entered a strange and unusual place, with bright lights. I walked down a long and illuminated path where trees grew gems. Rickshaws with soft, white leather seats carried infants in mid-air to a playground free from harsh sounds. I saw angels wrap their feathery wings around small, sweet-smelling bodies. Children and adults in all shapes, sizes and colours frolicked joyfully.

I felt a gentle hand shake my shoulder. 'Gwen.'

Curled into a ball, I opened an eye. My mother was folded over me.

Sleep never came easily again. The nights grew long. Every creak and thud were magnified and interpreted. My spirit companions flooded in, almost as if they had an open invitation. I didn't like them. They hovered, asking me to take messages to people for them. I didn't want to. I tried to ignore them, close my eyes. Pray.

Sometimes, on entering a place that I hadn't previously visited, I'd sense a weight or see the shape of a person.

There were so many other things my mother could have told me during these conversations that would have been far more useful to me, like how babies were made. Or why Anglo-Indians were so estranged from their fellow countrymen, but no, she chose to tell me this. Why, why this? How I wished that I never knew this information.

I had turned from a scaredy cat to a mini mouse – eyes darted, body shook, face twitched at everything that wasn't familiar to me. I was perfectly happy without this useless piece of knowledge. Now, I felt the need to scan everything around me – survey if it was real, not real, dead or alive, alive or dead. I didn't know the difference then; they all looked the same, spoke the same. The dead had no boundaries. They came at any time, invited or otherwise, but that in itself was not abnormal.

In India, it was customary for people to drop in for a visit when they wished. If it happened to be at mealtimes, they shared the meal. That became a key to me sieving out the dead from the living. The dead never had a place set for a meal, nor did they stay the duration.

Not conversing with unknowns I decided would minimise the chance of brushing up with a dead person. Push everyone away, keep to yourself, and keep the antenna on alert. Now, I knew that I was different from others.

I soon realised that to me people's thoughts were audible and often I saw their intentions in advance. Many dreams materialised. Incidents were realised ahead of their actual occurrence. I often received messages from the spirit world but it was rare for them to present in a straightforward way, in fact most came in a jumbled form that had to be untangled before it made any sense at all. At first, I didn't know how to break it down or that I was required to do that to understand its meaning. The one certainty being that I wanted no part of it. My world as I knew it was shattered. Prayer became my safe harbour. I never told anyone at school, or anywhere else for that matter, other than my mother. I was Between Two Worlds.

While growing up in India and being raised as Anglo-Indian, yoga wasn't something we practised or even observed anyone doing. I was oblivious to a tradition being carried out in the country in which I lived. However, I had an upbringing filled with prayer. God was a source of comfort and peace, no matter what prevailed, that had always been clear to me. Traditional Hindu mala beads had not been used in meditation, but my rosary beads were well-worn. My daily prayers were a form of meditation and concentration. My parents had taught me universal laws, what was right, what was wrong. Now, I consider, perhaps all the trees climbed, holes dug, limbo barres cleared, walls scaled and jumped, which also forced fresh oxygen into my blood, may have been my physical training. They didn't have the labels of yoga – asana, pranayama – but they happened on a road I travelled, alongside my caul gift.

Through Hindu servants, Anglo-Indians were familiar with the principles of Ayurveda, the knowledge of life, but then we didn't identify it by its name. Many an Anglo-Indian mother would have been offered buttermilk for good health and ladoos made from *ahaliva* by their ayah. God forbid the woman should find out it was Ayurveda the ayah was passing off to improve her lactation. Instead, the woman would have seen it as devotion from her servant, offering her a sweet. During the summer months, lassi (curd and water churned) was drunk to cool the body. Bitter gourd to improve the quality of blood, brinjal, eggplant to benefit the heart, methi, fenugreek, mace, saffron to name a few, would already have been used for health benefits. The severe itch that came with chickenpox or measles was soothed with neem or sandalwood paste.

Unknown to us, Ayurveda had been applied over the seasons to correct our doshas – *vatta*, *pitta* and *kapha*. Seasonal food and drinks were consumed to keep our bodies healthy and in rhythm with the seasons. During menstruation, women were advised to keep away from strenuous duties and remain isolated to rest – a teaching from Ayurveda's genital system and its claim that the body's system is weaker at this time, requiring care.

Had my family not migrated to Australia, perhaps I would never have had the opportunity to venture on the yoga path. It should have been easier for me from the time of my birth until my teenage years before I left India to uncover at least some of what all this meant. To the contrary, I was distanced from it.

In Australia, unlike my mother and sisters, all of whom taught Catholic scripture, I chose yoga. Unknown to me, my spiritual level of yoga had begun at my birth, hidden in my bones. A deep-rooted sense churning within. I had been given a clear path to travel this remarkable road on a physical and spiritual level, which has brought me what I needed, when I've needed it, be that a teacher, a special book, an individual, a group, travel to some place or an experience as a life lesson.

As a teenager, through my visions, I had worked out that unseen was not unreal. I had reflected on what was moral from amoral. And how I should live. What was true and what was false.

Being alone in Khajuraho had given me the time for self-reflection and aroused in me the distinctiveness of being connected to a higher source, where emotions and spiritualism, although clearly separate from each other, appeared to merge. It was not by serendipity that I was at the temples in Khajuraho alone. My yoga path had led me back to India

– an indelible filament, anchoring me here. The body I now stand in had changed and so had my mind.

My spiritual life is intricately linked with my relationship to God but has no link to the laws of the church. What the proclaimed servants of God do or don't do in his name is irrelevant to me. My true sense of purpose was not revealed to me as a child, but now as a grown woman, a wife and mother to two adult children, in a quiet village in India, the significance of my caul gift – a sixth sense – is revealed. It is about being of service. And I feel the true power of India within.

For the first time since becoming a yoga teacher, I feel the impact of why this path had been laid out in front of me and know that, although a proud Australian, my birthland is the integral spark to who I am. This now confirmed to me that, despite my British heritage, my Indian birthright must be acknowledged.

Previously, I hadn't considered this vital, but falling in love with my birth country and making this deep-rooted connection has fanned a hunch from a smouldering ember into a roaring fire.

Delhi, India's capital, is my next destination, a place of importance to my father, and the perfect place to visit a ministerial office to insist on having my Indian birthright conceded. I pray that the universe supports my desire.

13

Government businesses will close for the day within hours of my plane touching down in Delhi. And my initial thought is to rush over to the government office responsible, to have my birthright acknowledged, but I know at this hour it will be fruitless.

The driver of my prearranged car for the duration of my stay in the national capital looks official in a white suit with black and gold lapels. He is a tanned man, with squinting ebony eyes and a moustache that is twirled and tamed into neat points at the ends of his cheeks. He greets me. 'Welcome to Delhi, ma'am. Your first time here?' He loads my luggage.

'Yes, it is.'

'Welcome, welcome. A cold lemonade, ma'am?'

I prefer water, but not wanting to appear ungrateful, I thank the driver. I check that the seal is unbroken, and that it hasn't been refilled. Fetching a straw from my handbag, I draw in a refreshing mouthful.

'It is little late now, ma'am, and you have had a very long day, yes? But if you like, I can show you a few sights before I take you to your hotel in the city centre.'

I burn with desire for acknowledgement of my birthright, but also see the wisdom in my driver's suggestion in visiting a few places now. I can attend at the government office first thing in the morning.

'Thank you, driver, that is a good idea.'

A twenty-minute drive places us at a UNESCO World Heritage site – the Qutab Minar. A five-level minaret, seventy-three metres high, built as a victory tower to demonstrate Muslim dominance in Delhi after the defeat of Delhi's last Hindu kingdom. Its construction began in 1193 under India's first Muslim ruler, Alauddin Khilji, but was completed by his successor four years later. At its basement, I enter the first mosque that was built in India. And instantly I am taken back to the home history lesson my father had given following his initial visit to the monument. A sadness comes over me that Daddy has long passed and I cannot share this experience with him.

The minaret, a mixture of Hindu and Muslim architecture, is the result of Muslims demolishing twenty-seven Hindu temples and reusing their materials in conjunction with Islamic architecture in its construction. The lower floors are composed from red sandstone, with the upper two levels in marble and sandstone.

Nearby, there is an enormous iron pillar. The driver tells me of its legend – to make dreams come true, for those who wrap their arms around it. I think it's worth a shot, considering that tomorrow I will confront authorities to acknowledge my birthright.

Leaving this historical sight behind, we drive past the Birla Mandir Temple, one of Delhi's famous Hindu temples. I am whisked towards the city centre, with thousands of people, food stalls, three-wheelers, buses, cars and smog. We are forced into crawling pace, following the pageantry of a wedding procession ahead. I am fascinated by the coloured lights, and the generator powering them, together with a boom box belting out music, all being carried by humans, on foot. Drums beat, and odours from diesel to sweet marigolds lace the air. The groom, in a red and gold sequin studded dress-length long shirt and skinny white pants, rides upon a richly decorated elephant. Attendees matching his Indian attire, but less glamorous than he, hand up money to him, for prosperity in his new life, I suppose.

Nearing my hotel, I face a triumphal arch – the India Gate, inspired by the Arc de Triomphe, Paris, and built in its likeness. This confronting and sobering monument pays homage to the thousands of Indian soldiers who gave their lives fighting for the British Empire during World War I and, later, in the Afghan War. In all its vivacity, this city leaves me with a sense of history, mystery and romance.

My hotel oozes with opulence, solid mahogany furniture, padded in rich, red and gold silk. Paintings depict the Chandragupta Maurya, India's first rulers, as well as rulers from the near past, but there is no evidence of British rule.

At dinner, the in-house chef claims, 'A piece of Delhi resides within *chole bhature*', a rich and spicy chickpea and onion curry, eaten with baseball-shaped Indian bread. The fullness of the meal, together with the day's exhaustive events, form the perfect tranquilliser for a deep sleep.

Room service for breakfast will give me more time to prepare for my big day ahead. I slip into a green salwar kameez, pull back my hair and drape a dupatta over my shoulders. A glance in the mirror confirms that I look appropriately Indian.

Sipping Darjeeling tea served from a silver tea service, set on a matching tray, with cutlery securely enfolded in a white cloth serviette. I butter toast and spread a lavish layer of guava jam. My thoughts shift to my visa. Previously, the thought that they will want my maiden name to verify records of my Indian birth had not occurred to me. I steady a quavering hand. Is getting my birthright acknowledged worth the risk? What will India discovering who my father is mean for me? This thought weighs heavily on me. But now that I have confirmed that my soul resides in India, how can I allow myself to be deprived of something so important to me?

Two hours later, out on the driveway, I wait for my lift, somewhat earlier than I need to. Shafts of sun warm my shoulders and I soak in a myriad of people in their daily lives, catching transport, setting up daily business. And for a brief moment, the apprehension of my challenge today vanishes.

The driver arrives and greets me with a cheerful smile, '*Salam*, ma'am.'

'*Salam*, driver.'

A car door is held open, I climb in and my trepidation returns. The driver, astutely recognising my mood, remains quiet for the entire journey.

At the official visa office, I am ready to claw back my birthright. Staff at the counter do not give me a sideways glance, which validates that I do not stand out as anything other than Indian.

When an opportunity presents, in a voice laced with honey, I make my appeal. 'I only have a few days in Delhi while travelling in India. I wonder if it is possible to get an appointment to talk with someone today or tomorrow about my visa.'

'If you want to wait, maybe today.'

I have no inkling how long this wait may be but stay. Again, I review everything I may be asked, where was I born, went to school, when did I go to Australia…and my father's name. After an hour and a half, I am called to a counter. Behind it, a grey-haired woman wearing thick round metal glasses and a peacock blue sari, gives me a blank look.

'Thank you for seeing me,' I smile.

'You have a problem?' The woman eyes my Australian passport.

'Good morning. I am wondering how I can get a permanent visa to visit India in the future. I was born in this country.' I display my Australian passport, which says place of birth, Calcutta.

Her grim look tells me she has no sympathy for my plight. Without asking, she takes the passport out of my hands, looks me up and down and walks away. I lip-read her saying, 'Anglo-Indian.' Half a dozen bureaucratic eyes, the upper echelon perhaps, have been called upon to view this phenomenon, and intense scrutiny is under way. I wait at the counter for a few minutes, until I am signalled to 'Take a seat.'

My stomach is in turmoil. 'Should I wait or come back?' I ask.

'Up to you.'

'How long will it take?'

'A few hours, maybe longer.'

'I'll come back, but could I have a receipt for my passport?'

A filthy look accompanies an official paper.

Grateful that I have managed to secure an appointment today, I accept all that is being handed out to me.

The driver suggests we use the time to do a little more sightseeing and takes me the length of a lavish avenue resembling the Champs Élysées in Paris.

'Where are we?'

'Rajpath, ma'am. I told you before. You forgot? This is a grand avenue, ma'am, built in 1914 on a colonial scale. It links Indian government houses to India Gate.'

For a few minutes, I relax and enjoy the expansiveness of the large square with its many open areas and multiple courtyards, but without my passport I feel worried.

The driver picks up on my inattentiveness and decides on a cure-all treatment, 'I'll get you chai, ma'am, to refresh and make you happy again.'

In a few minutes, the lavishness of this grand avenue is out of sight and we have halted at a local market's tea stall.

A wooden crate is wiped off for me to sit. The chai wallah is in a blue-checked dhoti, his perspiration-stained singlet is pulled over a rounded paunch. In ceremony, he brews together tea leaves, ginger root, cardamom, cinnamon…the hot chai is then cooled to drinking temperature by being poured from one container to another a metre apart without a drop spilt. A metal tea strainer holds back the gritty ingredients when the chai is poured into a disposable *chatti,* clay cup. Once I finish my chai, I am at liberty to smash the *chatti* on the ground for recycling. The entire process is meditative.

In a serene state, I return to check on the progress of my visa request, all the while terrified that they will connect me with my father's escape out of India. The thought of a simple question, 'What's your family name?' being asked makes me light-headed and my shoulders constrict. For the next three-quarters of an hour, I stew on the same thought, over and over.

A thin man, with tiny oil slicks at the corners of his mouth, and a belt done up so tight that it ruches his black pants at the waist, signals me with the pen in his hand. His wide grin alludes me to good news and I am filled with confidence. 'Ma'am, it is not correct.'

'Thank you, no, it isn't. I was born here. I would like a permanent visa and appreciate if it can be amended.'

The tension that I have been carrying in my shoulders eases and is replaced with a twinge of shame for the many negative thoughts of interrogation that I had perceived would transpire during this process. All the answers to supposed questions that I had rummaged up, when did I leave India, why did I leave India…had been a clear waste of time and suffering. After all, I was born here and it is a reasonable request wanting my birthright acknowledged. And I am a little surprised how congenial they are being.

My gratitude overflows. 'Thank you, thank you. Should I wait for the correction to be made in my passport?'

'Ma'am, you don't need to wait, you can take it now. I am getting it for you.'

I have never encountered such efficiency with Indian bureaucracy previously. The competence dumbfounds me. My rating of this office gets a BIG mental tick.

'Much appreciated,' I gush with excitement, like a child who's been given an unexpected treat.

As he walks away, I consider my luck at getting this sorted with such ease, within a few hours and without a cost.

Anglo-Indians are the only community within India to have 'Indian' included in their community name. All other communities are identified by the state in which they live, Bengalis in the state of Bengal, Punjabis in Punjab… Anglo-Indians are also the only community within India identified separately in the Indian constitution. There should be no problem.

My passport is returned to me by a rotund man with a bald head, reaching up to the counter on his toes. The instant my passport is in my possession, he wags a menacing finger at me.

Filled with conviction, I flick open to the visa page and career out of control. 'Excuse me, my visa hasn't been changed to show permanent status.' I feel a knot in my throat, a tight muscle of injustice.

'Yes, ma'am.'

'No, it's not.'

'Yes, ma'am. There is a problem in your passport.'

'My passport?' I break into a sweat, 'What problem?'

'We cannot be certain that your place of birth is correctly recorded.'

And like a lioness, protecting her young, I pounce, 'Do you not consider that Australia verified that before including it in an official document, my passport?'

'You need to collect all the information required and then make online application.' He shrugs.

'Why? I'm here now. I want to do it while I am in the country in which I was born.'

'Yes, ma'am.'

'You can do it then?'

'Yes, ma'am.'

I pinch myself, to make sure that I am awake. 'Okay, I'll wait.'

'Yes, ma'am, we can't do it.'

'Can you or can't you?' I say, through clenched teeth.

'Yes, ma'am, we are not being able to do it. You have to do it from your country, online.'

Is this a joke?

Exasperated, I yell, 'And won't a final decision come from you, here in India?'

'Yes, we will need to approve.'

'And that can't be done while I am in India? Does it not make more sense that I do it while I am here?'

'We can't help you now, you have to provide proof that you are Indian, then renounce being Indian before we can make any changes to your visa.'

'Well, I'm Australian now. But I was born in India.' I wave my passport forcefully at him, 'And this doesn't prove that I was born here?'

'Yes, ma'am. It doesn't.'

This is surely a cruel joke being played on me and I guarantee the gods are still having their belly laugh.

My blood pressure rises. 'What the…?'

'When you go online, you can see.'

'You can't tell me?'

'Yes, ma'am.'

'What is it then?'

'You need to check online.'

'Get me someone in authority in this goddam office who I can talk to.'

'Ma'am, I am that authority.'

And, like a snail that has been stepped on, I feel my fragile shell crushed. Lost for words and fight, my prepared answers unused, I leave the office, knowing I have been beaten. By illogic. By bureaucratic idiots, idiots!

Out on the pavement, agitated, I shake with rage. My ride arrives. For a moment, I am distracted and amazed as to how drivers in India know when you are ready to move on, considering they have to park at some unknown place, some distance from the drop-off, without being notified of a time to return…perhaps another of India's mysteries.

'You are not happy, ma'am.'

The contempt I feel for the visa office exudes from every pore in my body like steam, so I am not surprised that the driver detects my disposition.

'Where would you like to go now, ma'am?'

'I don't care.'

'Sorry, ma'am. I am not understanding that.'

'Go anywhere you like.' I don't care where we go. I need some space to forget the last few wasted hours.

It is late afternoon when I return to my hotel. We must have driven around for a while, but on reaching the hotel, I don't recall anything that I was shown. I curl up on the bed and mourn the lack of acknowledgement. I think back to the day our family left India. Police lined the streets. The members of our family departing that day scattered throughout Calcutta. Perhaps acknowledgement of my birthright isn't worth it. I know the best thing for me do at this time is to connect with my family in Australia. I console myself and reflect on the joy and how lucky I felt the day I got the news, that we were leaving India for good.

14

Once I turned fourteen, it was a regular event for Hannah and me to attend early morning Mass on Thursdays – a regulated day off school. It was usual for us to leave home even before the sun was up. Church alternated between St Thomas's Church in Camac Street, Calcutta, near my godfather Dan's house, and Mother Teresa's Missionaries of Charity, the Mother House on Lower Circular Road. Following Mass, we did spiritual work at the place we had attended.

It was still dark when Hannah nudged me in bed. 'Gwen, we have to leave earlier than usual this morning, I need to drop in to see a woman before we go to church.'

We packed in haste a string bag filled with bread, milk and fruit from home supplies. At five o'clock, we were ready to leave on foot. We arrived at a makeshift cardboard street dwelling. The night streetlights were still burning. Roads and footpaths had been cleaned.

'What are we going to do, Hannah?'

'Wait and see, Gwen.'

Outside the dwelling, a woman sat on her haunches, cradling a baby with a head the size of a watermelon. It looked limp. I felt nausea rise in my throat.

Hannah walked up to the woman, handed her the supplies that we had brought. 'Do you want your baby to be in God's care?' she asked the mother in Hindi.

The woman, with tears in her eyes, raised her hand to the heavens, her sunken cheeks creasing into a smile.

Hannah took this as confirmation, poked her head into the lodging and picked up a white enamel tea mug. I soon got the idea of what was about to happen and knew that I better feel well again.

'Come on,' said Hannah.

We raced to a nearby *chappakal*. Hannah pumped the water and I held the mug under the mouth of the pipe. Water rushed out, bubbling over the cup, wetting my hands and shoes. Together, we carried the cup back to the woman and her baby. The mother held her baby's head towards Hannah, as instructed. From the cup, Hannah poured water over the baby's head, praying, 'In the name of the father, son…' and as one we said, 'Amen.' The child was now baptised a Catholic, and in God's care. The woman drew the baby close to her chest, wiped its damp head with the corner of her sari. She looked at us with smiling eyes, as if we were angels of the approaching dawn.

With the baptism completed, we hurried on to St Thomas's Church for Mass. Next, we did our regular dusting of the altar and pews, put flowers in vases, restacked hymn books. At Mother Teresa's place, the work was different – distributing food and clothing or whatever was required on the day.

At St Thomas's, following our cleaning and tidying, we retired to the sacristy. There, from unconsecrated wafer sheets, we pushed out circular indentations to be used as hosts for Communion. When we were younger, with permission, we took the surrounding pieces from the sheets and any hosts that were damaged in the process of being removed from the sheet. At home, Nelson said Mass, and placed the broken hosts on tongues. For the blood of Jesus, we sipped water or lemonade from a homemade paper chalice. The remaining hosts and remnant pieces from the sheet surrounds were eaten like crackers, chewing them with vigour because they were not yet the blessed body of Christ. But now, we politely left them behind.

On the day of the baptism, Hannah suggested, 'Let's go to Jimmy's Chinese restaurant for lunch.'

It was well before lunchtime when we arrived at the restaurant, but the owner Jimmy welcomed us in his changpao, a long gown, and pointed straw hat, puffing on a cigarette. 'Nice to see you again.'

I had never been in the restaurant previously.

We ordered wonton soup, noodles and chilli chicken. Hannah pulled two crisp ten-rupee notes out of her pocket, as if she were plucking flowers. It was hard to tell if Jimmy smiled or not, because he had a smiley face anyway. I never knew where the money came from, nor did I even care about it – maybe Hannah had saved up all my tram fares that she kept from me. From that day onwards, our visits to Jimmy's became more regular.

Jimmy was always delighted to make us anything we wanted. Occasionally, we had a few coins left over, which we spent at the *modi*. Not on the grains and flours he sold, but on boiled sweets and barley sugars from foot-long glass jars with aluminium screw-on lids. The *modi* put our purchases in small paper bags made from newspaper.

According to my parents, in the years leading up to India's 1947 silver anniversary of independence from Great Britain, there were regular upheavals and bloodshed. Work and lifestyle in India had taken a turn and, for Anglo-Indians, it was not for the better. Top positions had become a struggle to achieve, regardless of educational or social status.

Following independence, my parents, like many other Anglo-Indians, considered the prospects for future generations of our community would diminish. Being eligible for British passports, they had made a successful application to immigrate to England. Daddy then contemplated whether life for Anglo-Indians would be any different in England. In India, they were regarded as English. In England, would they be regarded as Indian and face the same problems? With that uncertainty, they remained in India.

More than a decade later, in the mid-sixties, despite the challenges for Anglo-Indians, my father reached the position of printer and publisher of Calcutta's most widely read daily newspaper, *The Statesman*, a position that would make him responsible for everything published within the newspaper and any litigation that came with it.

Mummy kept home, with six of their seven children. Their oldest child, Patricia, had married and no longer lived at home. Mary and

Catherine, next in line, were established in their chosen careers. Nelson, the middle child and only son, had commenced a degree in engineering. Hannah, two years younger than he, now sweet sixteen, was preparing for her final year of high school and Senior Cambridge. At fourteen, I was due to sit that exam in a couple of years. Alison, the youngest in the family, was nearing the end of her primary school years.

Daddy could possibly have found employment for the four younger ones when it came their turn to enter the workforce but, on further reflection, he and Mummy realised the limitations it would place on their children's professions.

Although England had been a natural first choice when a young and developing Australia was eager to welcome accomplished professionals, my parents considered this an ideal chance to emigrate. When it got down to it, Australia would be the better country; it had land, sunshine and opportunity.

The prospects for the future looked favourable. In the very late sixties, Patricia and her family journeyed to Australia. A few years after their departure, Catherine applied for immigration and was accepted. With their first grandchild and oldest daughter having already migrated and another daughter following soon, it became a significant pull on my parents' decision to apply for migration to Australia.

At dinner on the day that Hannah had baptised the baby and I had been her apprentice, our parents announced that the rest of our family would apply to emigrate to Australia.

I considered this good fortune, a direct result of saving the baby's soul.

'The baby had encephalitis. I am happy it is now with God,' said Hannah.

Soon, we too would be nearer to God, in the land of milk and honey, Australia. The news that we would apply to leave India forever was received with joy. This would definitely be a lucky change for me. 'Dead people, I am out of here,' I cheered.

A few years before the decision to apply for migration, the newspaper at which my father was printer and publisher reported and exposed politicians of a particular party in a cover-up. The party concerned denied the allegation and brought a defamation case against the newspaper. Because of my father's position in the company, he was naturally a key person. No one involved officially was permitted to leave the state, and undeniably not the country. From previous defences in such matters, Daddy had expected that a hearing would be complete within the next eighteen months and definitely before we would have news of our acceptance into Australia.

I check my watch. It is dinner time back in Sydney, and I hope that everyone will be home from their regular day. I need cheering up and decide not to mention the birthright dramas that I encountered today. It will only upset my family if they know and it is not the reason that I originally planned on visiting my birth land.

'Hi, sweetheart, I knew it was you when I saw a strange number come up,' said my husband, Gennaro.

'How could you be so sure it wasn't Telstra, Mumbai, giving you more value on your account?'

We laugh.

'Haven't heard from you in days. We thought you had disappeared.'

'I too feel as if I have disappeared,' but I stop short there. 'It's the time difference that throws me out. I'm fine and getting around. How is everything in Oz?'

'Same as usual for me. You know, the routine drill. I'm home alone at the moment. Kids not back yet. How's India?'

'India is amazing, magical, beautiful. You know I love Australia and am so grateful and proud to call it home but India resides in my soul. I don't know where to begin…there is so much for me to catch up on.'

'Do you need more time there?'

'I do but my visa will run out, so I'll have to return again and again. I still have places to visit in Calcutta. After a busy day, I've come back to my hotel for a rest. The timing was perfect, so I thought to call.'

We talk for a few more minutes.

'Okay, ring when you can.'

'Give the kids my love. Tell them all is well with me and I'll try them on their mobiles again in a couple of days.'

Calling home invigorates my spirit and once again I am ready to go into battle for my birthright. This renewed passion for India makes me wonder why I had returned to India on a tourist visa in the first instance.

We are at a time when the world is aware of India's technological growth, and I am certain that there will be no problem in requesting a laptop to be delivered to my room. The concierge is not certain the request can be fulfilled. I take a long deep look into my wallet and that hastens the probability a hundredfold.

I leave an envelope with baksheesh for the deliverer of my laptop and go to dinner. On my return a couple of hours later, I find a laptop set up on my coffee table. Excited, I turn it on and discover that the internet speed is dismal and, after many unsuccessful attempts, I give up.

Considering how fortuitous it is that I have already collected a couple of formal documents for my family tree from Chennai, I have requested others. Documents for my maternal grandparents would not be required. Women's heritage appears not to matter. I had a copy of my birth certificate back in Australia, along with other documents and, when I get back to Calcutta/Kolkata, I will arrange to get a baptism certificate.

My planned visit to the Taj Mahal is a few days away. I call my driver to let him know that I will be leaving Delhi soon, and would like to visit a few sights before then.

I retrace my father's footsteps through Delhi. At a street corner there is a snake charmer, with his *punji*, wind instrument, resembling a flute. Straight away, I recall the weekly visits that I had experienced when growing up in Calcutta.

In the same way that I had done decades earlier, I back away when two flared hoods, with sleek black scales, enticed by the movement of the flute, sway in hypnotic trance. Shining jewels, glistening and gazing directly into the eyes of its charmer, or so it appears. After a few minutes, the charmer gives a subtle and mysterious signal visible only to the cobras and together they lower into their containers and lids are secured.

Back in my childhood, the show didn't stop there. Canvas bags were untied, releasing more slithering reptiles, entwining around the charmer's arms, neck or coiled into his turban. The final amusement was a lesson to the troublesome boys who had been foolish enough to taunt the reptiles during the show or in a previous week. They would be given a dose of nuisance themselves – a sleight of hand trick sent a slithering snake up and down their shorts. High-pitched screams thundered and a commotion erupted as young boys fled the scene.

At Connaught Place, with its Georgian-style buildings, I wander its global chain stores, cinemas…on my way back to the hotel, stopping at the Sikh temple, Gurdwara Bangla Sahib with its golden onion dome. Staring into its reflective pool, I see my image – a woman who knows where she belongs and is determined to have that conceded.

If you are not born of another country in which you now reside, it is impossible to understand that no matter how much you love and are grateful to your adopted home, for its generosity and opportunity, a shred of you resides in your birth land – like the sun's gravity that holds the planets in its orb, a diaphanous thread never setting you free from the pull of your birth land.

The road to the Taj Mahal from Delhi is arduous, but well worth the misery endured to witness the riveting creation and monument of love. It takes my breath away and one visit will not suffice. I arrange to return the next day at dawn and dusk. For me, it becomes the perfect metaphor to signify my love of India.

My guide is eager to point out the missing gems and semi-precious stones from its inlay work, that he claims had been gouged out by the British. I discontinue listening to his history lesson.

I return to Kolkata on a warm winter's evening.

'Hello, Diana. I'm back.'

We relax with a cup of tea, and I can tell from her attentiveness to me that she is curious.

'Tell me all about it. Was India what you expected?'

'It was much more. I never anticipated that India would mean what it does to me. I learned a great deal about myself, and that India resides within me.'

'What do you mean?'

'My soul is here. By growing up Anglo-Indian, I've missed Indian culture and experiences.'

'But you are Anglo-Indian, British.'

At dinner, the conversation is non-existent. And I am excused for an early bedtime, on account of tiredness.

Back in my room, I call Melvyn to let him know of my return.

'How were your travels, Gwen?'

'Not long enough, but I have decided that I want my Indian birth acknowledged.'

Silence.

'You there, Melvyn?'

'Have you any plans for the next few days yet, Gwen?'

'I will be visiting my old school in Elliot Road tomorrow. I also need to get my baptism certificate from St Thomas's Church.'

'Gwen, shall we meet up at Flurys the day after tomorrow then, and take a trip to Alipore Zoo?'

'Sounds perfect. Ten o'clock suit?'

'See you then, Gwen.'

15

The morning following my return to Kolkata, I board the tram to Elliot Road, and go straight down the back. Women passengers look up at me while avoiding eye contact. In a T-shirt and jeans, I stand out like a goat in a herd of elephants. Detecting my awkwardness, a school-age girl wearing a burgundy-coloured salwar kameez and matching head scarf makes room on a nearby bench seat for me.

'*Shukriya,*' I say, nod and smile.

'You are welcome, ma'am. Are you visiting in Kolkata?'

'Yes, I am. I grew up in Cal— I mean, Kolkata.' I still find it difficult referring to Calcutta as Kolkata. 'I'm on my way to visit my old school.'

Men from their prime front section seats turn their heads in my direction. Females stare with pupils dilated.

The schoolgirl who gave me a seat adopts me into the sisterhood. 'My name is Parvsirka. This is my friend Fatima.' She gestures to her companion, in a white salwar kameez without a head covering.

'You are born in India, ma'am?' asks Fatima.

My response of 'Yes' gives special permission for more questions.

'How old are you? How long will you remain in the country? Are you married? Is he Indian?'

'I have a son and a daughter, both at university. I'm married and my husband is an Australian-born Italian. I have been in India for a few weeks and its almost time for me to go back to Australia.'

'Where did you meet your Italian husband, ma'am?'

'Australia.' I didn't feel the need to elaborate.

'Will you visit the Taj Mahal…?' Their eyes wide and shimmering like the ocean.

'I've already been to the Taj.'

'You are so lucky to see the Taj, ma'am. We live in this country and haven't seen it.'

'I didn't see it when I lived here, either.'

'Which school did you go to, ma'am?'

'Loreto Elliot Road.'

'We are also Loreto girls, ma'am, Loreto Sealdah. We are not in uniform today, because it is party day.'

'My older sisters went there,' I say.

The skin around Parvsirka and Fatima's eyes crinkle.

'School will close day after tomorrow. We are nearly at your school stop, ma'am.'

My heart sinks when I think that the school may not have time to find the information I require. 'Thank you.' I stand up.

The conductor reaches for the bell rope above his head, but Parvsirka jumps up, tugs on the rope and ding-a-ling chimes through the carriage.

'Thank you. Have a great party day, ladies.'

'We are getting off with you, ma'am,' says Fatima.

'Is your party around here?'

'No, we are taking you carefully.'

The girls each take a hand and together we walk past a vendor at the corner, weighing and bagging coal. Fully skinned goats hang from hooks outside the butcher. The apothecary, in addition to compounding medicine, now stocks bottles of nail polish and sticks of black kohl. Everything is exactly the same to me, except older and smaller.

When I see the green on cream school sign on a wall outside my old school gate, tears well. I wipe them away in a rush.

'You will be all right,' my two self-assigned guides reassure.

'We have to go to our school now.'

'Thank you for your kindness, ladies. I wish you both all the best.' And within moments, the girls are out of sight.

Reminiscing my school days here since kindergarten, I wonder if junior classes still line up under a tree for school milk scooped with ladles from aluminium *dhechis*, cooking vessels, into aluminium mugs for distribution. The milk was always tepid. I didn't like milk but drank it and felt sick inside.

I picture ayahs in white saris sitting together like pearls on a string, in wait for their charges to enter the lunchroom. When our ayah saw Hannah and me, she enquired as to how we were. '*Ke sa hai?*' Smiling, she took our hands, leading us to a table that she had set, complete with tablecloth.

Ayah put a serviette each on Hannah's lap and mine. She unpacked the tiffin-carrier, and served rice, lentils, curry, pappadums and rissoles made from potato and spicy meat. She brought seasonal fruit and insisted that we eat in front of her.

Many ayahs spoon-fed their kindergarten charges. But there was a group of children with no ayahs.

While we ate, children with no ayahs entered. They formed a queue at the back of the room and were each handed an empty enamel plate. They were given food from big pots, and moved onto long tables to eat. We knew they were sponsored to help with their education and welfare.

Once Hannah and I had finished lunch, our ayah wiped our faces and hands with a towel, which she had wet in one corner, and dried us with another.

A lifetime later, once again a darwan stands sentinel at the gate, reluctant to allow me entry into the school grounds.

'I'm an ex-student and now live in Australia. I want to visit my old school and I also need to talk to the administration staff,' I tell him, and show him my passport. Place of birth Calcutta, on a foreign passport, the cue. It works everywhere in India for me, except at the Indian visa office.

The gate opens enough for me to squeeze through. I walk across the playground at the all-girls school. Students are at play with basketball, netball and other games. Some students are seated on benches or concrete stairs in conversation and laughter. The regulated khaki and green uniforms in my days here have been changed to green and white.

At the office door, I talk to Shari in administration about school records and permission to walk around the grounds and rooms. She reminds me of a peacock in her distinctive glittery sari. The *bindu* centred at her forehead moves up to her hairline when she talks or smiles.

'It is the last day of school for the year, ma'am. We are very busy. I'll be with you as soon as possible. Please, come sit.' She shows me to a hardwood seat outside the office.

It was the last day of school all those years ago when Mrs Bernardino, my fifth-class teacher, chose me to assist her in preparing for our end-of-year party. Balls thwacked against walls and basketball backboards. I poured hotgram and chips into bowls, arranged sweets and cakes on plates.

My tummy felt uneasy. I excused myself and went to the bathroom. Five minutes later, at the bathroom sink, I see my reflection in the mirror, shaking and crying at the sight of blood on my underwear.

When I re-entered the classroom, Mrs Bernardino with her sixth sense smiled at me and walked me to the cupboard. She pulled out a floral strip of what appeared to be curtain fabric, dusted it, folded it twice into a long strip, handed me the wad. 'Line your drawers with these.'

'My drawers!' I stared at Mrs Bernardino, repelled.

Outside the administration office door, she whispered to Sister Marie Claire, our newest nun with rosebud lips, silky smooth skin and long, dark, eyelashes. Older girls in school said that she had been jilted, that's why she became a nun.

Sister Marie Claire put her hand on my head, smiled and looked at me as if she understood my plight. Had I been jilted? I didn't smile back. Nothing to smile about really – my drawers were thick and uncomfortable.

Everyone in the office stared at me that day, or I thought they did. Their chins drooped, the same way they did on the day the school called an urgent assembly, lined up all the students and walked us to the house next door. On the way to Mrs Deeth's place, we prayed the rosary.

At Mrs Deeth's front door, there were wreaths and sheaves of flowers – they had strong fragrances. My palms sweated, my knees felt weak and I wanted to cry, but held it back. At the drawing room door, we were halted.

Sister Marie Claire instructed, 'Please be very quiet.'

In procession, we filed past a black box. Within lay Mrs Deeth with eyes closed and a bloated face. She wasn't in her usual schoolteacher clothes, instead in a blue going-out frock. It was odd, because she looked pretty much stuck in the box and unable to go anywhere.

With thick drawers, I felt frightened, the same way as I did when walking past Mrs Deeth, in her box, three years earlier. Sister Marie Claire told me to sit on a hard wood chair while she telephoned my mother, murmured into the phone and hung up. I tugged on my fingers and wriggled in the seat.

Sister Marie Claire massaged her hands as if she were applying Pond's cold cream. 'We are getting a rickshaw to take you home.'

When I reached home, my mother was waiting for me. She rubbed my back in a circular motion. 'Don't tell the boys,' she said. Once inside the house, she ushered me to the bathroom.

I wasn't sure what I shouldn't tell the boys. An aluminium basin with steamy water was set up and there were fresh towels and a chunky bar of red Lifebuoy soap with its mild disinfectant smell. She handed me a pile of calico cloths, folded the same way the teacher had done and a bucket in which to place my soiled undergarments.

Confined to my room that afternoon, Ayah brought me lunch – chicken broth and *pish-pash*. At first, I was happy to be alone and read but hours later, I took a break and looked out the window. There was heightened activity in the front yard next door. I knew of the girl, about my age, who lived in that house but we had never met. I was curious that her window was surrounded with coloured lights, marigolds and jasmine. That girl's life was filled with celebrations, pujas and fireworks. Today she obviously had more fanfare. Lucky girl, was my first thought.

Cream canvas marquees with jasmine entwined around their posts and coloured flashing lights strung from edge to edge were enchanting. Into the marquees, servants carried wooden tables and bench seats. Outdoors, there was a clay oven and ovens erected from red bricks. Coal and cowpats added for fuel. Stainless steel cauldrons at the ready. Baby goats turned on spits. Servants carried in speciality sweets and baskets laden with bananas, guavas, star fruit, custard apples and mangoes. Vegetables were peeled and chopped. Prepared roti dough was covered with damp cloths.

Tethered in a corner, six white horses garlanded with orange marigolds, and red and gold feathers in their bridles, swished tails and pawed the dry earth. Musicians beat tablas, singers warmed their vocal cords and sitar players tuned strings.

I was immersed in the display when Mummy checked in on me.

'What are they doing out there?' I said, pointing into the yard.

'Ayah said the girl next door will have suitors. She too had the same thing happen to her today, like you.'

'What happened to me, her?'

'The same thing.'

'What's a suitor?'

'A man who wants to marry her. She will have lots of suitors come and ride on the horses. Her family will choose a marriage partner for her.'

My heart rattled; a train ready to derail. The girl next door was probably eleven, the same as me.

'When will she marry?'

'Soon.'

That was all the information I was going to receive for now. Once again, I was on my own.

I am not letting them get me suitors. I will not get married. That is all there is to it. I do not care what they say, I am not leaving here. This is my home and this is where I am staying. It was all that I could think about for the next few hours until everyone came home from school and work.

At dinnertime, I was out of isolation. Mummy cautioned me not to touch the food, especially the preserves. Nor was I to wash my hair or take a full bath for the next week. And, further to that, every month when this occurred, I was to make the same restrictions on myself. There was no explanation given, only instructions.

Following dinner, Mary took me aside and told me about what I then thought was an unnecessary burden, that I would carry for a very long time in my life. She showed me a packet of 'Angela', thick, six-inch cotton wads, small pillows to line my drawers. Monthly. Then, it occurred to me that a new ritual had begun in my life, but I didn't have a clue as to why or what. She did not talk about conception or babies. 'Baby' and 'pregnant' were not words that we were allowed to utter back then. There was no reason given, that was the way it was. At least at the end of my conversation with Mary, it was clear that I hadn't been jilted nor would I end up in a black box any time soon. Also, I would not have suitors parading for me.

Anglo-Indian females were free to choose their marriage partners when they were older than I now was. Of course, I could have been saved all that worry had I known that we did not follow Indian custom.

Ten, maybe fifteen minutes pass before the school office door opens. Shari, the office attendant, introduces me to two senior students, my guides for a school tour.

'Thank you. Would it also be possible for me to get some old school records?'

'That will not be possible today. Can you come back after the holidays?'

'Sorry, no. I won't be in India then.'

'You can leave the details, and payment for what you want.'

I write my details and give sufficient funds to cover the inconvenience and postage of records.

'We can show you around, ma'am. Is this your first time here?' ask the two young girls in unison.

'I'm an ex-student, from a long time ago. I now live in Australia.'

The girls' eyes widen and they give me glowing smiles, as if I am some extraordinary relic. Instantly, a crowd of students rally around us and there are numerous requests to take photos with me at various angles – standing, sitting, arms around each other. At the conclusion of the photography, I am given a tour of classrooms, the science laboratory and main hall. At the nun's refectory, the girls apologise that they are 'out of bounds'. I laugh at their words and remember when I was originally shown around the school as a small child how I had heard that the refectory was 'out of buns'.

Sincerely thanking them, I bid the girls a fond farewell. I catch sight of a girl not quite primary, not quite high school, writing in a colourful notebook on her lap.

I am taken back to when I was eleven years old and used my colourful notebook to write stories. A few school friends and I had joined together to initiate *Just for Fun*, a magazine. I provided life stories and jokes, the editorial team of five told me I was funny.

At first, the magazine was handwritten. Then Daddy taught me how to typeset the double-sided ten-page A5-size magazine at his place of business. Once mono copies were printed off, the production team, who also happened to be the contributors, editors and distributors, coloured in half the printed copies with colour pencils, to sell as colour copies. Mono copies cost five paisa each, which cannot even be converted into money today, and the coloured ones twice as much. I smiled at the thought of my writing career at that tender primary school age. The magazine got a write-up in the *Junior Statesman*.

Although drawn into the memories of school here, I must make my way to St. Thomas's, my baptismal church, for yet more records.

16

The sun is descending from its midday position when I leave the school and stride to my childhood parish church. I arrive at Camac Street fifteen minutes later. My godfather, Dan, once lived on this street. Outside his place I stop, as if in respect of his stately figure and considered words. Winnie, his widow, has long left this city.

Hannah and I had a standing invitation from Auntie Winnie for breakfast on Thursday mornings, following our church work at St Thomas's. Even on days when Auntie was not available, the servants had strict instructions to provide us with breakfast when we turned up.

As soon as Auntie's servants heard Hannah and me on the stairway, with its signature odour of gas that came from the cooker, they held a door open for us, guiding us to high-backed padded chairs at a table set with a white damask cloth, matching serviettes, polished silverware, gold-rimmed white cups and saucers, teapot, milk jug and sugar bowl to match. Freshly squeezed orange juice in crystal glasses was at the ready.

When seated, our feet did not reach the floor and swung like pendulums. Auntie's ayah placed a serviette on my lap and another on Hannah's. Cook fussed around, preparing eggs whichever way we fancied, together with toast, selections of fruit conserves and our favourite Amul cheese. The cook also skimmed layers of cream from boiling milk and beat it to a consistency thick enough to spread on toast or to eat with a spoon.

How much we enjoyed the special treatment. As a child, I had not appreciated the many treasured moments stored in my memory. But now, on my return to India as an adult, so much of me is desperate to belong to this country again. I hope that I will be successful in collecting all the relevant information to make that a reality.

At St Thomas's Church, the black cast-iron gates are shut. And I am deeply disappointed. But there had been a time when I had wished that the gates would be locked and that Father Picachy had been called away.

That was the day my legs felt like cotton wool as I walked down the church aisle. Light streamed through the leadlight windows behind the larger than life size crucifix, illuminating the red paint smeared on Jesus's wounds. I bowed my head, genuflected and made the sign of the cross. Once in a seat, I recited the *Credo in Deum* – 'I believe in the Holy goat, umm ghost…'

The confessional queues were long. The Easter congregation had assembled to declare sins, seek forgiveness and be spared the fires of Hell.

On the first day of religious instruction, when preparing for the sacrament of first Holy Communion, Mother Superior, our Irish Catholic school principal had forewarned us of the gates of Hell. She explained the difference between venial sins and mortal sins and the torturous fate that Hell would bring if we committed a mortal sin. Sister Bernard, Sister Cecelia or the parish priest himself made up for what she didn't cover.

On the actual day of my communion, dressed all in white, ready to receive Jesus for the very first time, I felt so pure. My soft brocade long frock was gathered at the waist. A floral headpiece of rosebuds held a short tulle veil that tickled the nape of my neck. Kneeling at the steps of the altar for Communion, I recalled all rules of host etiquette; not chewing it, not letting it touch my teeth or stick to my palate. Once it was placed on my tongue, I swallowed it and felt proud.

At the conclusion of Mass, first communicants returned to their individual schools, where breakfast was served. Group and individual photos were taken, after which we were free to go home.

Back in my neighbourhood, I went from bungalow to bungalow announcing my communion and showing off my rosary beads and prayer books. Now that I had received Jesus, the neighbours told me that I was a good girl, and gave me a few rupees and a pat on the head. By the time I got home, I felt a headache coming on.

The Easter following my first communion, waiting at church for my confession to be heard, I remembered what Mother Superior had reminded us of time and time again – in order for an act to be a mortal sin, we had to have full knowledge of its sinfulness. We had to know that 'it is wrong and be aware that we are committing the act.' Eating the forbidden apple in the Garden of Eden was a sin committed by Adam and Eve – it stained our souls but at baptism it was washed away.

To be sure that I had chosen the correct sin to confess, I went through the ten commandments, 'First commandment, I am the Lord thy God…', pausing at the sixth commandment and mouthing the words slowly, 'Thou shall not commit adultery.' There was no mistake. Yes, I had definitely committed a mortal sin. This was not one of those venial sins that could be glossed over. Trembling, I reached into my pocket, pulled out my rosary beads and did the rounds.

At the marble altar, candle flames made small quick movements and pearly beads of wax dripped down. Their fragrance, mixed with that of recently burned incense, filled the church with a smell of sacredness. On the walls, partially rolled marble scrolls, showed Jesus's crucifixion. He carried the weight of a cross on his back, a crown of thorns on his head. His blood-strewn face made me queasy. Fear engulfed me. My knees dropped to the rough hardwood pews and I felt a burning sensation that crept up my thighs. The Hell fires had started. Now, I was truly sorry that I had committed a mortal sin.

Father Picachy made his way out of the sacristy. Bowing his head at the main altar, he made the sign of the cross. With each step he took towards the confessional, his white cassock swayed. Rosary beads the size of walnuts tied at his waist made a tick-tick, tick-tick sound. A time bomb counting down. A bush of grey eyebrows hooded his eyes, and his white beard with some black hairs mixed in trailed over his chin. When he passed me, he nodded his 'how-are-you-my-child' nod. I acknowledged him with a nod, lowered my gaze and shifted on my kneeler – a sinner, on my way to Hell, fire licking at my heels.

Father entered the confessional box. A minute later, two people in the front row rushed to open the doors on either side of the box and entered. In the ten minutes one of them had taken, my rosary beads had become hot in my moist palm.

A confessional box became free and I entered. In front of me was an oblong rattan screen not much bigger than a shoebox. It had a solid timber window behind it that was shut. I could hear voices on the other side of it, but the words were unclear. I hoped that the person in the other confessional had a lot of sins to confess. It would give me more time to prepare myself. I knelt on the cushioned kneeler below the screen and slipped the rosary into my pocket. I wiped my hands on my skirt, ran a finger over the screen, and pressed my ear to it. Mumbles.

My mind filled with a picture from Daddy's book *Dante's Inferno*, where Satan was trapped in Hell. How God, as punishment, banished him out of Heaven to an eternity in Hell without forgiveness. Now I, a mortal sinner, would be sent away to join Satan. The door on the other side of the confessional creaked. I squeezed my eyes closed and again wiped my sweaty palms on my skirt before bringing them together in prayer position. Seconds later, I heard the timber window on my side slide open. I opened an eye and saw Father's seraphic face crisscrossed like rattan. I closed my eye and made the sign of the cross.

'Bless me, Father, for I have sinned. It is one week since my last confession.'

'What sins have you committed, my child?'

Father had a lot of children; some were even older than he was. Why did he call everyone child? I shifted on the kneeler and it groaned.

'Go ahead, child, what did you do wrong?' asked Father.

'I wasted my dinner, didn't finish homework for my Bengali tutor. And I didn't share sweets with my sister.'

'Is that all, my child?'

'No, Father. There is more.'

'God is forgiving, my child. Tell me everything now.'

'I didn't want to do it, I knew it was wrong, Father, and I shouldn't have done it.'

'Tell me, my child, and then I can absolve and give you penance.'

'A mortal sin, Father. The fires have started to burn me up. I am being swallowed into Hell.'

'What have you done? Tell me now.'

'I broke the sixth commandment.'

'Pardon?' asked Father, his voice ricocheting off the confessional walls.

'Adultery,' I murmured.

'Pardon? Speak up, child.'

'Adultery.' I raised my voice a little.

Father sounded as if something was stuck in his throat. He was making gagging sounds. 'I don't think so, my child. How old are you?'

The Hell fire inside me burned. I had sinned. Why was he saying I didn't do it? Why does he need my age? 'Yes, I did. Seven years old,' I sniffled.

'You didn't commit that sin.'

Now, I had enough tears to fill a bucket. 'Father, I…did. I DID.'

Writing a rude word about my older sister on the bedroom wall was an adult thing. Children are not supposed to say rude words. 'Adultery, adultery,' I wept uncontrollably.

'Say three Hail Marys for your penance. Eat all your food, share with your family and do your homework.'

'What about my mortal sin, Father? The fires, Hell…?'

Father raised his right hand and waved it around, '*Nome ne padre, a spirito, a sancto. Amen.*'

I wanted to make the sign of the cross, but my fingertips only managed to jiggle across my forehead and down to my chest. Was I forgiven? What about Hell?

'God bless you, my child,' said Father, his voice cheery. The window on my side of the confessional box shut.

Slowly, I stood up, wiped my eyes, smoothed my skirt, and rubbed my cool knees. My insides felt like I had just eaten chocolate, warm and sweet. There would be no Hell fires. Getting out of that sin was easy. Maybe it was okay to commit adultery again.

I smirk at the memory of my innocence, and how we were taught words in religion at ages when we could not understand their meaning, when an elderly man opens the black cast-iron gates. He looks dutiful in a crisp white shirt, and black slacks.

'Good afternoon. I was wondering, is the parish priest available?' I ask.

'Perhaps I can be of some assistance? I am Rodger, I help out here.'

'I need to get a copy of my baptism certificate, Rodger.'

'Oh, I cannot help with that. I will check if Father is in the vestry.' Rodger invites me to spend time with God in the church, while he searches for the parish priest.

St Thomas's, a colonial-style church with a Doric-columned portico, topped with a short octagonal spire, was founded in 1842. It had been my family's parish church until we moved away from Elliot Road to the area where Diana now lives. Our entire family had received many Catholic sacraments in this solemn and holy place.

I enter an empty church with the sound of joyous but thunderous music. Perhaps the organist is practising for an upcoming wedding service. The abounding harmonious vibrations uplift and remind me of my parents' twenty-fifth wedding anniversary celebrated at this very church. The all-male choir at St Xavier's, where Nelson studied, lent their solemn voices on that happy day. My heart soars at how proud my parents had looked on that day, when our entire family, relatives and friends joined in the merriment.

Light streaming through the church's stained-glass windows draws me back to a similar striking light a decade earlier and the day Daddy died. It was my one-at-a-time turn to visit him in the intensive care unit, when I got a strong feeling that he was about to pass. The rest of the family were directly outside the ward awaiting their turns.

'My father is about to die. Please ask the rest of the family in,' I said to a nurse nearby.

She looked at me, narrowing her eyes, but I insisted.

We all gathered around Daddy. Uninterrupted fervent prayers continued for his safe onward journey.

The nurse edged her way through us and checked his vitals. 'He's unconscious, he won't respond any more,' she said, and backed away.

At that precise moment, a ray of white light streamed down from the ceiling and covered his entire body. And he opened his eyes for a brief moment. As they closed, a silver stream, about the thickness of an umbilical cord, glided out of his mortal body and travelled up into the white light.

Holding his hand, I followed the conspicuous beam and whispered, 'Leave some of your energy with me, Daddy.' A feeling of strength and peace encompassed me. And there was no immediate grief, instead a moment of ecstasy, knowing that my father was moving into a higher place.

At his funeral, many people expressed their credit to him and Mummy for getting them educated or paying medical expenses when in India.

I am startled by a tap on my shoulder. Rodger has crept up beside me.

'Father Rodrigues, the parish priest, and the only one who can provide you with the document you require, cannot be located right now but he is nearby. Can you wait?'

'Thank you, I can wait.' I don't plan to leave if I have the slightest opportunity of getting documents.

Then, the guilt of defying my mother consumes me. I want to believe that Mummy would be pleased that I am fighting for my birthright, all the time knowing that she would prefer if I left my visa with its status as 'tourist'. Within the church, the overarching strong scent of incense, evokes the day Mummy was farewelled from her earthly life.

17

Mummy's coffin lay at the bottom of the church altar, swathed in lily of the valley. Altar boys, robed in white swung censers. The smoke caressing sunlight spilling through leadlight glass windows. The church looked warped.

On a Sunday, two weeks earlier, Catherine, Alison and I had accompanied our mother to lunch at the Sydney Casino. It was an unusual choice for our mother, who never gambled.

'I've never been to the Casino. All my neighbours talk about it,' said Mummy, dressed in a white spotted top and navy skirt. Her hair had been styled earlier that morning; the grey rinsed out for another six weeks. A swipe of Revlon pink to the lips, a dab of Joy to the wrists. As she stepped out in her latest fashion purchase, low-heeled navy pumps with a white leather stripe, I suspected that Mummy ran a private fashion parade in her bedroom, with her many nice frocks.

At the casino, lights overpowered. Gambling rooms droned like bees swarming. Poker machines delivered coins, ching ching, ching ching. We walked across purple carpet flecked with orange to the restaurant, a glass-enclosed room with water views. A waitress in a heavy floral brocaded gown showed us to a table. Yellow and red Chinese lanterns highlighted sumptuous dishes on glossy menus. We chose chilli-fried crab, special dumplings…finished with mango pancakes. How different it was from the usual Sunday afternoons that we spent at our mother's place, eating cucumber sandwiches and hummingbird cake, and drinking Darjeeling tea.

Following lunch, we watched blackjack and roulette players peel off notes from wads of cash, throwing them down on game tables in exchange for plastic chips. Mummy fooled around, putting a dollar's worth of five-cent pieces into a poker machine. Cigarette smoke choked, bringing our visit to an end.

I had driven everyone to lunch and afterwards dropped my sisters off at their respective homes before returning Mummy to the retirement village in which she continued to live following Daddy's death, six years earlier. The sun was setting as I drove my black BMW into the village.

'I hope the neighbours see me… Sometimes they act as if they are the only ones with money,' said Mummy.

'Don't worry about them. They probably have nothing better to do.'

Mummy didn't seem to care about my response. She touched my arm and looked at me intently. Since a child, I could recognise that look of worry in my mother's eyes.

'Gwen, please go. Don't walk me up to my apartment. It's getting dark, go home. Today was wonderful, thank you.' Her troubled tone was all too familiar.

'Mummy, I am going to make sure you are in your apartment before I leave.'

'Truly, Gwen. I will be okay.'

We kissed on her doorstep and I walked downstairs. I was a grown woman with children and Mummy still worried about me being out after dark. The air stilled, and I got the distinct scent of roses surrounding me. Daddy loved roses. I smiled and soaked in the aroma. Parents – forever watching over you.

The previous Sunday, Alison and I arrived in the car park together. Catherine's car was already there.

On entering Mummy's apartment, Alison and I looked at each other with raised eyebrows. The mahogany china cabinet had its glass doors flung open, as if a sale were about to happen.

'How are you, Mummy? Catherine?' Alison and I chorused.

We all kissed.

'Why the open cabinet?' the chorus chimed.

'Sorting…things out.'

'What things?'

Without a response to the interrogation about her china cabinet, with trembling hands Mummy served afternoon tea.

'You all right, Mummy?' Once again, the chorus struck up.

'Oh, yes. Would you like cake?' She sliced up generous servings.

Catherine didn't touch her cake. Alison and I polished off a huge slice each.

Mummy smoothed a crease in the tablecloth. 'What do you want from my china cabinet? Choose anything that doesn't have a dot on it,' said Mummy to Alison and me. She handed us each a sheet with ten red and orange sticky dots, respectively.

'Why are you giving things away?' I asked.

'No, not giving away yet, just getting things in order.'

Alison looked in the direction of the cabinet. 'I don't care what colour dot is on the dinner set, your good one, the fine china with the twenty-two-carat-gold rim, hand-painted flowers at its rim, it's mine.' She turned away from the cabinet, contented.

'I don't want anything from the cabinet, but if you could leave me the family papers, I would be happy,' I said and glanced at the cabinet, a sea of multicoloured dots.

In a nearby garbage bin, a sheet with two yellow dots remaining was discarded.

'We are only doing the cabinet today,' said Mummy.

'Okay by me.' I stared into the bottom of my empty cup.

'So, when are you planning on leaving us? Get an order, did you?' I laughed. 'You can't die any time soon. I don't think you'll ever die. You still have a mountain of photos to put in albums and I have already told you that you can't leave until they are sorted out. It's your job.'

'Come.' Mummy led me to a pile of photo albums on her bedroom chest. 'Look, they are all done.'

That knocked me for six. 'The jewellery?' I asked.

'Done and labelled.'

'But we will never locate the key and it will remain in the safe forever,' I teased.

'That has all been taken care of...'

I was out of this game.

'Forget that idea, Mummy. You are not going anywhere yet,' said Alison.

'When the Lord calls, I want to be ready.'

'Yes, yes,' I said in mockery. 'Let's talk about something more imminent like your seventy-sixth birthday at the end of the month. What would you like to do?'

'Let me think about it. We can organise something next week.'

Mummy switched on the television. 'I want to see how the preparations for the Sydney Olympics are progressing. It's only weeks away from the opening ceremony.'

'Mummy, Alison and I have to go,' I said.

Kiss, kiss. We departed.

Eight days later, outside a hospital, the eerie whines of ambulance sirens were unnerving. Alison and I had waited for almost an hour since we received a phone call telling us to meet the ambulance in which our mother was being transported. Alison kept watch while I went to admissions.

'I am not sure that anyone by that name has been admitted. Also, it's possible that it takes a while for the computer to show up a newly admitted patient,' said the triage nurse.

'Would she have come through here if she came by ambulance?'

'Guess so. Take a seat. We will let you know.'

Outside the building, from my mobile phone, I called all the local hospitals. No one with Mummy's name had been admitted.

Alison's eldest daughter, Tracy-Maree, arrived. The two kept guard, and I made another visit to admissions.

'Please check again. I have tried all the local hospitals. She has to be here,' I said.

The triage nurse flipped up a page and read an orange highlighted line at the bottom of it. She swung the book around. 'Is this her?'

'Yes, it is. She's here then?'

'Yes.'

'Of course, she is,' I said, under my breath. 'What's her condition?'

'Have to get the doctor to talk to you. He's treating her at the moment.'

Alison entered the hospital building. By now, more family members had made their way to the hospital. Three-quarters of an hour had passed since we had last asked after our mother's condition and approached the triage nurse.

I lost all sense of patience. 'We need to see our mother, please!'

The triage nurse didn't look up at me. Instead, she picked up the phone. Alison and I got permission to enter the emergency room. It had that sterile, recently bleached stench. We poked our heads into various cubicles. Bodies lying on beds were attached to various cords, monitors and drips. Finally, we found our mother propped up on pillows, wearing an oxygen mask. A young nurse, who looked as if she should still be in school, was taking her blood pressure.

'What's her condition?' Alison took control, as she did with things medical.

'I don't know exactly, but the doctor isn't worried about her condition.'

Alison reached over and placed her hand on Mummy's forehead. 'She's burning up. We need cool water and washers,' she ordered the nurse.

'I feel nauseous. Can I lie down?' asked Mummy.

'No, Mummy, better to sit up,' I said.

A doctor approached us and the strong fragrance of roses clung in the air. I looked around – no flowers in emergency.

'Dr Cheng,' he introduced himself, without looking at any one in particular. 'I am looking after Mrs…' he looked up the chart, '…your mother.'

'Daughters.' I identified Alison and me.

Alison's olive skin had drained of colour. Was this washed-out girl my sister? Then I caught my reflection in a nearby windowpane. Nothing a good rest can't fix, I consoled myself.

'Your mother presented with chest pains. We will keep her overnight to monitor her condition.' Dr Cheng signalled the nurse, who brought a vial.

'Droperidol, to stop the nausea.' Dr Cheng injected Mummy in the arm, smiled and left.

Six hours had passed since Mummy had been admitted. A serving of mashed potatoes, green pureed something and clear soup was delivered on a brown tray. I fed her two spoons of soup, which was all that she could stomach. Alison fixed her bedding. We left the room to give other family members a turn.

Catherine and I demanded permission to stay overnight at the hospital.

'You can't stay. Go home, get some rest. We have given her something to help her sleep,' said the attending nurse.

That night, I tossed and turned in bed. My husband was interstate. My body ached from fatigue and my eyes were heavy with lack of sleep. A bitter taste crept in and out of my mouth, its acidity burning my throat. The scent of roses filled my nostrils. I bolted upright. The feelings and smells collided. My bedroom ceiling became a stage of floating shadows. I shut my eyes, prayed.

I awoke with sunshine on my face and was surprised that I had slept through the alarm clock. I dropped my daughter, Chantal, off at high school and was on my way to the hospital, when my mobile phone rang.

'Your mother's enzyme results are back.'

'Who am I speaking to?'

'Doctor… Your mother has suffered a massive heart attack and we need to do an angiogram. We need permission.'

'I don't know what that is, doctor. How urgent is the test? What will it do? I will be in the hospital in ten minutes. Can it wait till then?'

'Yes, but not much longer.'

I called Alison, our home-grown medical guru. 'Can you ring the hospital, and deal with this. I don't understand all this medical stuff. I'm in my car, the traffic's horrendous, and this sounds serious.'

'I'll take care of it.' She hung up.

A road that I travelled every day had now become unfamiliar to me. I stopped and cried, composed myself then continued my journey.

On reaching the hospital, I saw Alison and Catherine waiting outside Mummy's room.

'There's a nurse in there,' said Alison.

The three of us discussed the angiogram. As soon as the nurse left, we went in.

'How are you feeling, Mummy?' asked Alison.

'Okay.'

The nurse returned swivelling six pills in a plastic cup – one pink, one blue and Valium. She boasted her knowledge of the other four white tablets.

'What are they for?' I asked.

'Sedatives, to keep her body calm during the procedure.'

'Procedure?'

'Yes, your mother signed her own authority form for the angiogram.' She turned her head to face Mummy. 'Take your glasses with you. You can watch it on the monitor,' said the smiling nurse as she left the room.

We three daughters looked at each other, raising our hands and shoulders.

'Mummy, do you want to pray before the procedure?' I asked, pulling a green covered Bible from my handbag, a birthday gift to me earlier that year from Mummy. The four of us began to pray. Realising that I had chosen a prayer for the dying, I improvised the prayer for a safe medical procedure.

'God bless you,' we said in turn.

An orderly dressed in white scrubs waited with a gurney to transport Mummy to the hospital theatre.

Catherine put Mummy's glasses in her hands. 'Put them on. You can check out your insides when they appear on screen.'

We walked beside the gurney to the theatre's entrance. The orderly bid us adieu.

'See you in a while,' we said in turn and kissed Mummy on the forehead.

It was a warmer than usual winter's morning and we decided to sit in the outdoors section of the hospital's café. Patients in wheelchairs, hooked up to intravenous bags, smoked cigarettes and drank coffee. Pigeons hovered around for scraps.

'Take the whole muffin, you greedy birds.' I tossed it on the ground. It wasn't going to reach my stomach anyway with all the churning that was going on in there.

Catherine's husband joined us. He bought us another round of tea. The sunshine was pleasant until a cloud came over the sun, as if a hand had shaded a face. A cold wind whistled. Uneasy, I looked at my watch – twelve forty-five. Our two-hour waiting stint was almost over.

'Let's go inside. Mummy should be back soon,' I said.

In the waiting area, we flipped magazine pages, paced the floor, waiting for permission to see Mummy. Another hour passed, still no Mummy. Alison and I went to the nurses' station.

'Excuse me,' I looked at the name badge, 'Sister McQueen,' I said.

Sister McQueen's glasses sat at the tip of her nose. She looked at us over the top of them.

'When do you expect our mother, room twelve, to be back from her procedure?' I asked. 'It's been three hours. We expected to see her sooner.'

Without acknowledgement or expression, McQueen pressed a few buttons on the telephone. '…when will she? Ah, yes, yes, okay.' She hung up. A blank canvas. 'The doctor is coming down.'

'Did everything go all right?' I enquired.

'A bit of fluid on the lungs. The doctor will be down. Use the nurses' station. Make yourself some coffee.'

It was then that I should have known that something had gone very wrong. Alison and I went back to the waiting area and informed the rest of the family that the doctor was coming. We then rang our other four siblings, alerting them that we were uncomfortable with the nurse's response. We tried Hannah for half an hour but could not reach her. Still no Mummy or doctor. We went back to the nurses' station.

'Excuse me, sister. It's been almost four hours now since the procedure. Where is the doctor?' I asked.

'Not here, still? They have been working on her. I'll check again.' We got a glance in acknowledgement. She picked up the phone, looked up at us, 'He's coming.'

My son, Daniel, had come to the hospital after university. Now, we were a party of six.

'What's going on, Mum?' asked Daniel.

'Wish we knew, my boy.'

'There are so many of you. When the doctor comes, it will be easier to talk to everyone together and answer any questions that may arise,' said McQueen. She ushered us into a room.

It was small. Dark.

I felt shaky and my palms were damp.

I startled back to the present when Rodger taps me on the shoulder. 'Gwen, I have located Father. He's on his way soon. I can show you the way.'

'Thank you, Rodger.'

Together we leave the church and take a dozen steps under the archway that separates the church from the vestry where we are headed. On one side of the archway, manicured gardens, with schoolgirls farewelling each other for the holidays. At the other end, traffic crawled in keeping with my mood.

'This way, Gwen,' Rodger opens the sacristy door, the same one through which Hannah and I had once gone to sit, pushing out hosts from wafer sheets.

Wooden drawers stacked upon each other lined the pale cream walls of the cold and uninviting room.

'Sit down, Gwen. Father Rodrigues will be with you soon. Excuse me,' Rodger leaves me alone in the room.

And his words jolt me.

'Sit down,' McQueen had said in the darkened hospital room, a few years earlier.

But I didn't want to sit. Alison followed me out of the room and we stood in the corridor. A few minutes later, two men in their late thirties, one blond, the other dark, roughly the same height, walked towards us. They looked as if they had a problem holding their heads upright.

'Do you think they are the doctors? Perhaps we'd better get back in the room,' I said.

Alison shut the door behind us.

There was a knock. I saw the handle turn. The two men who we had just seen entered the room, clearing the doorway by a foot. The blond one had his fingers clenched so tight that his knuckles had turned white. The dark one, with cropped hair and sunken eyes, had pallid lips for someone with his colouring. The two men never looked directly at anyone. I smelled roses again, fidgeted with my bracelet.

'Sorry it's taken so long to come and to talk to you. We did everything we could,' said the blond one.

If the other one said anything, I didn't hear it.

Words churned in my head, as if they were dregs being swirled in a teapot before being tossed. I was on my feet. 'What do you mean? Hh-hhas our mother died?'

Alison and Catherine stood up too. 'Is our mother dead? Is our mother dead?' We screamed in unison.

'Is my mother...?' Catherine sank in a chair.

I saw Alison's daughter, Tracy-Maree, restrain her mother's arms.

'You said the procedure...' Alison's voice faded to a blur.

The hazy voices filled my headspace and left, filled and left. I felt

Daniel's strong hands around me. I used to hold him tight like that when he cried as a baby. How I loved my children. How my mother loved her seven. I felt the years now slip away. Reverse. I circled, curled and heard the whoosh in my mother's womb.

Not true, not true – whoosh, whoosh. That damn doctor is talking through his hat, I thought I said.

'Mum, Mum.'

I heard Daniel's voice, distant. I looked up at the ceiling – flaking.

'Oh, my Mum,' he said.

'This can't be. Can't be. A big mistake,' I said.

'No mistake, my Mum. A blood clot lodged in Nana's aorta.'

'Nonsense. Where is she?'

Hannah arrived, carrying a large bouquet of red roses. Someone approached her. I saw her clutch the bouquet tightly and crash to the floor.

A nurse came into the room. 'In a few more minutes, your mother will be brought back into the room across from this one. Does anyone want a Panadol?' She put a tray down on a side table, with a jug of water, drinking glasses and Panadol. Did she think an analgesic would fix all of this?

'Gwen? I am Father Rodrigues. Thank you for your patience,' says the swarthy priest, with dark wavy hair, stubble for a beard, and square, thin-rimmed glasses.

'That's okay, Father. Thank you for seeing me without an appointment.'

'So, you live in Australia now?'

'Yes, Father, I do.'

'You want a copy of your baptism certificate. Yes?'

'Yes, please.' I hand him a slip with an approximate date, being two months after my birth date and a Sunday.

'I think we can manage that easily enough.'

I feel relief in his words. Father moves in a casual way towards the brown drawers, checking labels as he moves. Finally, he places his plump fingers on a large leather-bound book with a gold-embossed pattern and two stripes on one side. 'This one should have it.'

He opens the thick book to the month that I have indicated on the paper to him and pivots the book toward me. 'Here, you have a look. See if you can find it.'

I hover my finger over the page of hand-printed names and dates. With the utmost care, I turn a number of pages in this artefact, viewing the names of many families we had once known in this parish. I see my family name, and a record with my given name on it, and feel an adrenalin rush. My eyes cloud. A record of me in this country – I see my father's name, followed by my mother's listed as the birth mother. My heart rattles. I struggle to hold back tears, but the tide breaks. I hasten to wipe them away on my sleeve.

Back in a cold hospital room, years earlier, my tears had leaked onto and stained my mother's sleeve when she lay without a blanket covering. Silent. Still. Her face serene, her ashen lips slightly parted. I lay my head on her chest and put my arms around her.

'How are you, Mummy?' I asked, knowing full well she could no longer respond, but hoping I was wrong.

Mummy had given years of service to her church parish and naturally on her passing we informed her parish priest, Father Burton, and asked him to come and bless her body. On his arrival, he looked solemn, and proceeded to give a blessing for the sick. No one corrected him, and when he left, we all took a Panadol. And called the hospital chaplain.

Although the chaplain had no background with the woman who lay silent and still, he took over the prayers. His words were consoling and he gave a Catholic blessing for the dead, inviting each family member to sprinkle holy water on Mummy's body. We lit candles, picked the petals off Hannah's red roses and covered Mummy with them. Their scent overwhelmed. At first, we talked in hushed voices, so as not to disturb her, and later on in a tone that we hoped she would join in.

Five hours passed. Nelson arranged for Mummy to be taken to a private morgue until her funeral arrangements could be made.

'I've found the record of my baptism, Father Rodrigues,' I say, my voice cracking.

'That is very good. Do you need a drink, Gwen?'

'No, no thank you, Father.'

Father rummages in his pocket, creases forming on his forehead. He continues tossing belongings in a nearby desk drawer, then produces a fountain pen. In neat and careful script, he reproduces my baptism certificate.

It was four days since my mother passed. It was also the day that Catherine and I had an appointment to visit Father Burton for funeral arrangements. Alison couldn't accompany us, because her youngest son, Peter, wheelchair-bound with muscular dystrophy, was unable to access the vestry with no ramp.

At break of dawn that day, I heard my mother's voice. 'Gwen, I'm fine. Daddy is with me, my mother, Nana and my grandson, Wiley too…'

I felt the gentle weight of my mother's hand on my head to comfort me by running her hand over my scalp, the same way she had done when I was a child. On this occasion, she was comforting me by telling me that she was with relatives who had passed, especially her grandson, Wiley, who had passed as a young man, a few years earlier, under difficult circumstances.

'Oh Mummy, please stay…' Fragrant roses cocooned me and I sobbed into my pillow.

'Teresa's daughters?' Father Burton cleared paper bundles from chairs. 'Sit,' he gestured. 'The…arrangements?'

'Yes, Father, we will want a requiem Mass on Friday morning. And how long a eulogy can we give?' I asked.

'Friday. Yes, ten o'clock.' He flicked through a black, bound diary.

'Also, Adam, one of her grandsons will play his guitar. Teresa was a musician in her youth,' I said.

He held up a page from the diary with his index finger and thumb, and glared at me, 'This diocese does not allow eulogies, candles are forbidden, and no, no, you cannot have a guitar playing in church.'

'Pardon me, Father, no candles in church?' I said.

He noted something in the diary.

'Father, our mother was a woman of God. She has served the church her entire life. And, she has been a eucharistic minister for over twenty years.'

'No and no.'

'OK, I'll organise a service in the park.' Could I do that? 'And Father, you do accept the responsibility that her family of almost forty people may never return to the church?'

Catherine's face was puce with embarrassment.

'Let's go,' I said.

'You can say a few words. It must reflect her faith, nothing else,' Father Burton said, shutting the diary.

'I'll say a few words, all right,' I said.

'I wanted the ground to open up and swallow me when you challenged him,' said Catherine, as we walked back to the car.

'How dare he, how dare he?' My chest was caving in.

The following day, I went with Catherine to Mummy's apartment in the hope of finding my mother's spirit there. It was the first time that I had visited her home since she had been admitted to hospital, five days earlier. On the kitchen bench sat a cauliflower, beans and a half-chopped carrot. Catherine tidied up the kitchen. I wasn't interested in tidying. I needed to communicate with my mother and hoped she would oblige.

'She doesn't know that she's dead, or she would have come back here,' I said. As a child, she herself had told me that I talked to the dead.

Surely, I could talk to her. I was certain that a love bond made on earth continued into the hereafter. I knew it didn't disappear just because someone died, but I couldn't make contact with her.

Days after the altercation with the church, family and friends filled the church pews. In procession, Mummy's grandchildren, Daniel, Chantal and Sharon walked with Tracy-Maree and Kelly-Ann, who flanked their brother, Peter, riding in his wheelchair. Adam strummed his guitar as they entered the church, carrying candles ablaze. Hemmed in grief, Alison and I followed.

Once we were all assembled, Mary led the opening hymn, 'Come as you are…'

Nelson, being Mummy's only son, was nominated by family to read a succinct eulogy and tell how today, as her devout commitment to the Legion of Mother Mary, Mummy rested in her religious cloak, which she had preserved since she was fourteen years old.

Outside the church, from a dowel cage, I released seven white doves, one to represent each of Mummy's children. The flock circled the steeple, then flew away in different directions. A horse-drawn hearse carried Mummy to the crematorium chapel. As the thick smoke swirled from the chimney, the family accompanied Bette Midler, singing 'Wind Beneath My Wings'.

Although I got my way and, as a family, we gave Mummy a fitting and deserved farewell, the whole incident turned me away from the institution of church. I lost faith in a church that had no care, sympathy or regard for a loyal parishioner who had devoted her time and energy to it. I embarked on a new phase in challenging the church. I believe in a supreme being, and not necessarily by the name of God or Jesus, because I know first-hand there is a spiritual world, and something greater than me.

Father Rodrigues is waving the recently completed certificate to dry the fresh ink. Placing the document into a white envelope he asks, 'Will that be all?'

'Thank you, Father, that will be all.' I make an offering for his effort, and leave feeling as if I have struck gold – place of birth recorded as Calcutta, India, and baptism date.

Out on the street, rickety food stalls, made from wooden frames, are roughly draped in canvas. From them, spicy aromas float on a wave of fresh steam, fashioned by the nearby dhobi, laundry men, sprinkling water on garments and pressing them with coal heated irons. Familiar memories.

The sun blazes down on me and with a second wind, I navigate the traffic chaos, clutching my white envelope.

18

As prearranged, Melvyn and I meet at Flurys on Saturday. I fondly recall that, while growing up in Calcutta, the Swiss teahouse was one of the finest establishments for European confectionery. My family had frequented the place on many occasions, in particular in the year leading up to our disappearance from India. Mary, loaded up with funds from Daddy, often treated us to its many delicacies, following a day of shopping, for linen and fabrics to be sewn into dresses, shirts and trousers; and shoes of varying sizes, to get us started in Australia.

In keeping with tradition and in memory of my chocolate-loving mother, I settle on a cake dripping in Swiss chocolate. Melvyn chooses something less indulgent as we sip on Darjeeling tea.

'How was your visit around India, Gwen?'

'Enlightening, Melvyn.'

'How so?'

'There was so much of India emotionally and physically I didn't know about. And I realised that a large part of me is still here. I intend to apply to have my birthright acknowledged.'

'Doesn't your passport do that?'

'Insufficient, as far as India is concerned. I think I have a fight on my hands before the Indian visa office accepts that I am Indian.' I almost hear my mother rejoice at this admission.

Melvyn looks at me, with confusion in his eyes. 'You should let it go, Gwen. Let's make our way to the zoo.'

I am shocked at Melvyn's upsetting remark, but let it pass and push my empty cup away. 'Yes, let's go.'

Arriving at Calcutta's Alipore zoo with Melvyn feels unnatural. When our taxi arrives at its entrance, nostalgia from my childhood surfaces again, transporting me back to a memory of when I was five years old. It was an annual Boxing Day picnic tradition for Anglo-Indian families and their close friends. That day, my family of ten plus servants were joined by Beryl, Cliff and their nine children.

Busy hands unloaded car boots. Boys tucked bats and balls under arms, balanced blankets on heads. Girls swung baskets to and fro, packed with nets and celluloid dolls. Small children cradled fluffy teddy bears. Adults assisted servants in unpacking tiffin-carriers, portable stoves, pots, thermal flasks and cardboard filled boxes. Vendors at the entrance slid thumbs across a comb's plastic teeth, twang, twang, twang. Newspaper cones filled with peanuts, butterfly hair clips, bamboo slithering snakes and coloured plastic bangles with gold around their rims, all offered for sale.

A man with sucked-in gums and salt and pepper unshaven cheeks tapped the heads of faux-fur tigers making them bob and squeezing the sides of monkeys until they squeaked. '*Boney, boney,* please, ma,' the man pleaded with Mummy to give him his first sale for the day.

A passing bus belched smoke as Uncle Cliff shaped his hands around his mouth, and bellowed through the mock megaphone, 'Today, we have come to visit our relatives in captivity.'

Everyone laughed, and I joined in but didn't understand the joke.

Nearby, the acrid smell of dung fires fuelled the air. Mummy pulled a purple glass bottle from her handbag, poured liquid from it onto her white lace handkerchief and dabbed her forehead and neck. The fresh smell of lavender escaped.

Melvyn and I leisurely stroll past hawkers selling various snack foods, clothes, and plastic or wooden animals. Buying an Indian flag, I wave it as an expression of being Indian. I stop to browse at handmade jewellery and Melvyn gently takes me by the arm. With my head still turned back admiring enamel filigree, he leads me away.

Then I am reminded of when I was a young one here, dawdling on the pavement near black plastic flooring purporting to be a shop. The vendor showed off soapstone idols. 'Varuna, first god,' he said, selecting one mounted on a stick, vigorously shaking it. He picked up a pot-bellied statue with four arms and an elephant head. 'Ganesha, good fortune god.'

Curious, I leaned in for a closer look.

A hand grasped mine. 'Don't go near those things. We don't know what they are for.' Mummy dragged me away with my neck still craned in the direction of the community of gods readied for sale.

Melvyn and I walk to the ticket box. Throngs of people are clamouring, and I picture Daddy and Uncle Cliff a long time ago, at the front of the ticket queue, holding rupees at what I perceived then was the outside of a cage.

I had run away from Mummy to join Daddy. Standing beside him, I thought about how the Lilliputians must have felt around Gulliver on his travels. I tugged frantically on Daddy's pants leg and he swept me up into his arms.

Inside the cage stood a man. At his chest height, there were metal bars, with a semicircle space cut out at the base, and a bronze dish facing outwards. 'Name of school for excursion discount, please, sahib?'

'No school, just two families.' Both daddies laughed.

'Sorry, sahib, I am thinking it is a small school.'

Daddy pushed money through the half circle to the man. In exchange, back through it the man handed Daddy a pile of blue and orange pieces of paper.

'Daddy, Mummy will be cross if you give the man money and only get small pieces of paper back,' I said.

'Gwen, they are tickets for us to visit the zoo.'

Daddy was struggling to handle all the tickets and I was being jostled around, when I noticed little wooden boxes behind the caged man, stacked with blue and orange pieces of paper (...tickets) in neat piles.

The caged man gave me his one-tooth smile, 'Going in zoo today?'

He scared me and I shoved my face into Daddy's vest and was glad that the man was in a cage.

We returned to the group and I saw Mary. 'Is the man in the cage a rel-a-zive like Uncle Cliff said?'

'That's not a cage, it's a ticket booth, and no, the man is not a relative. Uncle Cliff was making a joke about animals being our relatives.'

'U-huh.' A smile crept across my face and, now that I understood Uncle's joke, I looked forward to hearing it again and seeing more rel-a-zives.

The two families gathered at the big gates and the daddies handed out tickets. The big people got orange tickets and the children blue ones.

A man in a turban at the entrance said, 'Ticket please.' He had a saffron cloth wrapped around his beard. He tore each ticket in half, kept one half and returned the remainder to the ticket holder.

I didn't want to have my new ticket torn in half and hid it in my handkerchief.

Hannah saw what I did. 'If you don't give him your ticket, he will not let you in the gate with us,' she said in her bossy voice.

She was only a very little bit bigger than me and I was used to being bossed around by her. I ignored her. But then I noticed that the man had a *kirpin* dangling from a belt at his waist. I wasn't sure if he would use his sword on people without tickets.

I ran up to him. 'Here's my ticket.'

He smiled. As he tore my ticket in half, he wobbled his head from side to side. I scuttled back to Hannah and gripped her hand.

Everyone held someone else's hand – a human chain entered the zoo. We found our picnic spot and spread our blankets. I pulled my handkerchief out of my pocket and wiped my shoes clean until they shone.

'Cliff, how about we have a game of cricket?' Daddy suggested.

Both men rolled up their long sleeves. A cheer went up, and there was a dash towards the cricket pitch with bats and balls.

Ayahs lit portable gas stoves, heated pot-roasted chicken, duck and pork. Vindaloo and jhalfrazee, an Anglo-Indian speciality made from leftover lamb, with chopped potatoes and onions, stirred with spices and rolled in the warm flaky pastry of parathas. Bologna, ham off the bone and Nana's special salted meat were spread on plates. There were shortbread star-shaped biscuits with shiny silver cachous on top. I licked my lips when I glimpsed sugar-coated kalkals and Christmas cake. Mummy and Nana helped the ayahs fill enamel plates for lunch until they brimmed. Auntie Beryl took care of her two youngest children, who were crying.

The aroma of food had already delivered the message to the fast bowlers before I called, 'Lunch is ready,' to the rest of the fun-seekers.

Nana poured homemade nimbu pani, the juice from fresh lemons stirred into cool water and tempered with sugar for the children, and steaming hot tea from thermos flasks, or bottled ginger wine, also homemade, for the adults.

The sun directly overhead prompted Mummy and Auntie Beryl to shade their babies with large black parasols. One of the babies awoke with all the chaos of lunch and Ayah rocked her back to sleep.

Melvyn and I visit a very different, updated zoo to the one I remembered. Adwita, the Aldabra tortoise, believed to be the world's largest tortoise and brought by British sailors from the Seychelle Islands in 1876 as a gift for Lord Robert Clive of the East India Company, had died a few years earlier, at an age of over two hundred and fifty years. It was odd, but I felt its loss.

'I was disappointed when I read news of the giant tortoise's demise, Melvyn.'

'Nothing lives forever, Gwen.'

'I know, but it would have been one of the original creatures that I would have witnessed together with my entire family, when in India. It would have meant something to me.'

Melvyn looks skyward. 'It was quite a surprise when you all left India. I mean, we knew you were accepted into Australia, but had no idea when you finally left.'

'There were a few legal obligations that my dad had to undertake on behalf of the company where he worked.'

'Is that so?'

'It was typical Indian bureaucracy and playing the game carefully, which would otherwise have ultimately impacted the entire family. Overtly advertising our departure would have been as foolish as these silly creatures.' I point to the chimpanzees and, as if it were happening now, I hear Uncle Cliff's announcement on the day of our zoo visit.

'Time to visit relatives.'

Daddy, Mummy and Auntie Beryl gave instructions as to whose hand you had to hold while visiting the animals. Nana remained with the ayahs to look after the belongings.

'Here's a good specimen of a relative.' Uncle Cliff pointed to a cage.

The chimpanzees squealed and threw their banana skins at the naughty *chokras*, teenage boys, who had scaled up their cages, mimicking and annoying them. Some of the boys in our family group scratched themselves under armpits and jumped up and down, mocking the animals.

I trip on a small dirt track and falter.

Melvyn darts over, 'You, okay?'

'Sure, didn't see the mound.' But it reminds me of flutters I got on that Boxing Day visit to the zoo with Uncle Cliff's family years earlier.

That day, far back, I had hoped for a fun day seeing all the creatures in my zoo book. But for me, once the fluttering began, I fretted. I often got that feeling before something unpleasant happened. I had looked around for Mummy. When I caught sight of her, I raced over and wrapped myself into the folds of her floral flared skirt. I decided not to tell Mummy what I felt today, because I knew that if I told her about these butterflies in my tummy, her face would turn chalk-white. But Mummy was not fooled.

'What is wrong, Gwen?'

'Nothing, Mummy,' I cried.

Mummy unravelled me from her skirt and bent down as she made the sign of the cross. 'Please God, protect us. I know that this child has an almost clairvoyant intelligence. What's going to happen?' Her fingers trembled as she fondled the gold crucifix dangling around her neck. 'How will I ever help link these two worlds for you, Gwen?'

'I want to go home,' I bawled.

'She's tired,' Mummy said aloud and gripped my hand firmly.

As we got nearer to the King of the Jungle, I decided to keep my eyes downcast as I approached His Magnificence. Daddy gave a lesson on lions.

As soon as he finished talking, Uncle Cliff's megaphone voice announced, 'On safari to the jungle tigers.'

When we stopped to view the tigers, my stomach started doing somersaults. It was a common occurrence for zoo animals to be taunted by visitors. That day, *chokras* climbed over the mesh fence that separated the tigers from visitors and, to provoke, they poked thin long sticks at them. One of the tigers paced near to them, flexing its gigantic stripy tail. 'Tiger, Tiger,' they called and poked. Uncle Cliff and Daddy chased them away and alerted a zookeeper.

I squeezed Mummy's hand. She bent down.

'There's blood,' I said, pointing to the mesh fence and bars on the tiger's enclosure.

Mummy put her hand on my head and squeezed firmly, her face colourless.

'Why is there blood, Mummy?'

'There is no blood, Gwen,' she whispered, staring at the bars. 'I place my trust in God.' I saw Mummy bite her lower lip.

The afternoon sun was hot for a winter's day and the area reeked of feline urine. I covered my nose.

'The smell around here is making Gwen nauseous,' said Mummy. 'We have to move away.'

Meandering along the path, Melvyn and I arrive at the elephant's compound. The large bristly, grooved, loose-skin animal is a favourite for me and a totem of extrasensory perception.

'Do you think elephants have melancholic eyes, Melvyn?'

I wished I could touch an elephant, and spot one with a painted trunk – pink and purple, encased in white painted diamonds tumbling to the ground.

If Melvyn responds, I do not hear him. Instead, I reminisce a day long gone, when, Mahout, elephant keeper, asked Daddy if the children wanted a ride on Rani, an Indian elephant, whose name meant queen.

Rani had long, thick eyelashes with worried eyes that I thought were very small for her large body. Then, I had pondered on a queen with dispirited eyes, concealed in grey wrinkled skin.

Daddy rummaged in his pockets for paisas and handed the money to Mahout, who then allowed the family's children to feed Rani peanuts and bananas. Peeling the bananas, she flicked skins out of her mouth, crunched up the peanuts and discarded the shells. Mahout rested a ladder up against her side and told us to scramble up into the metal box that was on her back. On low benches, covered in orange and green velvet, Hannah and I sat alongside other children.

Mahout coaxed Rani with sugarcane sticks in preparation for the ride. Unexpectedly, she trumpeted loudly. *Chokras* fled, taking with them hair that they had pulled out of Rani's tail. Mahout gave chase.

Mythology deems the connection between Heaven and earth is the elephant. An elephant-hair bracelet is believed to bring the wearer good luck and protect them from poverty and sickness.

On his return, Mahout stroked Rani. 'I am sorry, they are bad boys.'

My tears flowed because the *chokras* were unkind to Rani.

Bossy Hannah looked at me. 'If you want to get off, you can't. Daddy has already paid.'

Mahout sat up close near Rani's thick neck, clutching an iron claw; occasionally, he used it to steer her in the required direction. She strolled, unconcerned, using her long nose to break small branches from trees, shovelling them into her mouth. From the box in which we sat, I could touch the high tree branches and was sure that I could reach the sky if I stood up, but that wasn't allowed. Each time a branch swung in our direction, we screamed and once when we did, Rani stopped. She raised her trunk in the air like a periscope and swivelled it. I felt the tremor in Rani and knew that she hadn't stopped because we screamed. She and I had a precognition. My butterflies were awake again!

The ride stopped and Mahout blew a whistle. Shaking his head, 'Elephant ride finished, getting off everyone, getting off, getting off. Bullock cart will come soon,' he said.

We groaned that the elephant ride had stopped so abruptly but had no choice but to ride back in a bullock cart, which wobbled, crackled and creaked but also turned out to be fun.

Unloaded from the cart, I overheard a man tell Daddy, 'Trouble in the zoo, sahib.'

I was unable to recall anyone by that name but felt sure that Daddy would know who 'Trouble' was. Why else would the man tell him?

'Melvyn, do they still allow children to have elephant rides in the zoo?'

'Not sure, Gwen. We don't come to the zoo any more unless we have foreign visitors.'

Is he referring to me as a foreigner? I feel slighted at his remark but once again let it slide.

Daddy and Uncle Cliff talked, but I couldn't hear what they said. Then Uncle Cliff hurried everyone to the nearest shelter. And the two men left to investigate.

I turned to see a hundred pairs of iridescent blue-green 'eyes' all looking at once. Twinkling tail feathers fanned out, elongated aloft, in courtship glory. A national symbol of India. A crest atop his head, his royal-blue body illuminated against his brilliant plumage, an extravagant display. The peacock stood still as if allowing time to be admired.

Intimidated by all the 'eyes', I turned my back on them and looked straight into Hannah's eyes.

'Why don't we visit the reptile house?' said Hannah.

'No. Mummy said to stay together.'

'We will be together,' said Hannah, and off we went.

A few minutes later, we entered the building. We walked around tapping the glass on cabinets to see if anything was within. Sometimes, the cabinets were so high that I could not look inside them. There were a couple of open tins with brushes and rags nearby. Hannah was elsewhere in the room.

'I found a tin to stand on. Come over, you can stand on one too,' I called in a loud voice.

My new-found stool was fleeting. It tipped and varnish ran across the floor. As luck had it, I did not fall into the varnish but my shoes were a sticky mess. Hannah must have heard the crash and ran over. She reached me when the stench of varnish had got to me and I vomited – over her shoes. I left her and ran out but looked back to see if she was following me. Instead of Hannah, I saw a sign outside the building, 'NO ENTRY'. I was screaming for Mummy and not paying attention to where I was running. I darted straight into a group of men in khaki uniforms. They looked as if they had misplaced something. I ran around them, found Mummy. Amidst chaos, an ambulance siren blared, and people were running. When I caught up to Mummy, she didn't even ask about my shoes.

Daddy and Uncle Cliff came back to the group. Hannah had caught up with us. Ayah hauled us both and our smelly shoes to a nearby water pump. When we got back, the picnic had been packed up.

Daddy rolled down his sleeves, and hurried us along, 'Come children, time to go, time to go.'

Uncle Cliff didn't make any megaphone announcements. Instead, he hoisted one of his young children onto his shoulders. Then, the adults played Whispers. When Mummy got the whisper, she reached for a nearby bench with one hand and held her head in the other.

At dinner that night, Daddy told us that a tiger had taken a swipe at a *chokra* when we were on the elephant ride. Mummy put a hand over my mouth.

Recalling the tiger incident reminds me that my premonitions had begun when I was a small child, and also how much my mother had taken heed of my forewarnings. For a few moments, I try to force myself to divine whether I will be successful in attaining recognition of my Indian birth, but I know that it doesn't work that way. Visions for me can't be forced. They are random and more often than not, even when they do come easily enough, require some deciphering.

'Why don't we visit the reptile house, Gwen?' asks Melvyn.

Although I had no forewarnings today, I decline. 'My time in India is drawing to a close, with only days left. I should get back to Diana's. Thank you, Melvyn, for walking some old ground with me. I promise I will return to India.'

'It's been such a pleasure to see you, Gwen. So many fond memories.'

On our way out of the zoo, I am surprised that Melvyn doesn't comment on anything we have done today. He is more interested in the past.

'How and when did your family actually get out of India, Gwen?'

I look at him and feel the muscles tense in my face.

'You probably don't remember too much about it now.' He hailed a taxi.

'I remember the day I left India as if it were yesterday.'

19

Melvyn is not about to let the interrogation go. 'What gave your family the upper hand?'

'When we applied, Australian immigration policy required migrants to be distinguished and highly qualified people. My father's qualifications and experience, and those of Nelson's, fitted the conditions for us to be accepted. Also, my father had already secured a position from India with a company, Carmichael of Stanmore. Stanmore is an inner-city suburb of Sydney. One of Sydney's universities had also considered offering him a lecturer's position in engineering. We were all fluent in English and had been to reputable schools.

'Patricia and her husband had guaranteed us accommodation on our arrival, which was mandatory, in addition to my father securing work. It was compulsory that all members of our family accepted into Australia pass strenuous medical examinations, in order to rule out anything from poor eyesight to severe and chronic illnesses.

'Mary, as you know, remained in the family home. Eleven years later, she wanted to join us. Australia's migration policy had changed considerably by then and my husband and I had to undertake a financial sponsorship for her and her family. This meant we accepted the entire liability of all five members of her family from accommodation to medical and any other needs they may have had. In addition to that, it was essential for her and her husband to have jobs guaranteed. Hannah procured one for Mary's husband, and the electrical engineering company that I worked for offered to employ Mary on her arrival. I then spent excessive time in the offices of politicians, pleading the case to grant them entry on family tie reasons. Fortunately, they both managed to secure work immediately and did not need to use the guarantees that we had arranged.'

'But how did six members of your family leave undetected, Gwen?' asks Melvyn.

I frown. 'Do you mean, the actual day we left?'

'Yes, I am intrigued. I recall coming to a farewell party at your house in the heat of a summer's evening but you never left then. You were all around for months following the party, then vanished overnight.'

'It was a difficult and chaotic time, Melvyn. We couldn't publicise the exact date. It had to be kept low-key. Following final confirmation of our acceptance into Australia, Daddy resigned from his position. His company understood that we were leaving the country in the very near future. It took five months following that to get all our affairs in order. There were cars and property to dispose of, so transactions were happening. School transfer papers, domestic servants to consider. Furniture, linen, clothes, shoes…were bought, and a container, the size of a small room, was filled and shipped to Australia.'

'So why the secrecy?'

'Around three or four years before we left, a court hearing was pending in regard to a charge for an article being published in the newspaper. My father was responsible for its publication. No date had been set for the case. No one involved was allowed to leave the country.'

'Why did your family accept and book tickets to leave then?'

'With only two months left before our Australian visas for permanent migration lapsing, it was impossible to delay our departure, regardless of the court case. Everything had been arranged and a decision had to be made.'

'Who helped with your departure then?'

'Mr Ventura, a travel consultant, had become somewhat a fixture in our home in the months leading up to our emigration. He made all the arrangements to ensure my father got out of India undetected.'

'Weren't your family concerned that he might alert authorities?'

'No, my parents trusted him.'

My thoughts move away from Melvyn and I go back to the day when I left India as a teenager.

Three days before our departure, my father's office alerted him, as a friendly caution, that the court had issued a warrant for his arrest. He was not allowed to leave the state or country. Although my father's presence was required at court, the case was not an extraditable offence, but we had to be very careful. I don't recall being privy to much of those preparations, not all the intricate details anyway.

With six members of the family having to leave undetected, the operation was delicate. The previous night, we had to separate into the homes of our closest confidants. Although Mary had decided to remain in India, she accompanied us for our overnight stay in the home of a male friend of hers, who she had previously suggested to Mummy.

Mummy, her mind filled with the undercover arrangements of leaving, had agreed to Mary's suggestion without question. Also, that day, Mummy had her head buried deep in the bottom drawer of her dresser. She often kept money in that drawer but she couldn't find it. It was baksheesh, six hundred thousand rupees, twelve thousand Australian dollars. She and Daddy wanted to make certain that the servants had enough money after we had gone. Servants did not have bank accounts and cash had to be available for them. My mother did not find the money that day, but retrieved it the next and left it to be distributed after we had left. None of the servants, except for our driver, knew that we would all leave the next day.

No one would have given a second thought to seeing us out with Mary who, more often than not, assumed responsibility for the younger children. Mary took us with her on the mornings that we caught a tram to school, when our driver, Aladdin, had to take Daddy some place and did not get back in time for us. We rode together on the same tram as she did for work and she ensured we got off safely at the school stop. She also accompanied us to church, the movies, shopping, checked our homework and even disciplined us. On her paydays, we could always look forward to ice cream, chocolate or some other treat. When we were sick and absent from school, she wrote our absentee letters, advising that we were 'indisposed'.

Aladdin had driven us to the airport on many occasions, most notably when Daddy had an early morning flight for business and it coincided with our school holidays. It was invariably at the crack of dawn that Hannah and I sat rugged up in the back seat, alongside Daddy, Nelson in the passenger seat. Once Daddy had been dropped off, Aladdin took us through the city for a magic ride.

As the day's first rays of light tinged the city, street sweepers were active. Vendors opened shop shutters at their places of trade and commenced their early morning *puja* on home altars – offerings of food and sweet-smelling incense were placed at the feet of deities. Other ritual prayers and chants were performed to bring blessings for the new day. Aladdin took us for an early morning breakfast treat before the city buzzed with commuters, traffic, sales of newspapers, market stalls, fresh fruit carts and more.

The day Aladdin drove us to the airport for the last time, he didn't tell us one of his usual funny stories, nor did he pull up at a street stall and buy us steaming hot chai in an earthenware vessel, or *bhakakannis*, a flat and flaky pastry cooked with ghee. Despite cold air being blasted out from the air conditioning in the bottle-green Dodge, he wiped sweat from his brow. In all the years that he had been our driver, he had never been so uneasy at the wheel. He was almost a member of our family, except for the fact that he was not Anglo-Indian and had never crossed the threshold into our home.

I knew he would miss Nelson when we were gone but wasn't so sure about the others. Nelson wasn't in the car with us the day we left.

'Aladdin, will you miss us when we are gone?' I asked.

His voice quivered as he wiped sweat from his brow, 'Yes, *baba*.' He always referred to all of us as *baba*, child.

His constant dabbing worried me and I hoped that he was not ill again, like when he had tuberculosis and coughed and shivered with fevers. At his diagnosis, our whole family got tested, but luckily no one had contracted the disease from him. During this time, naturally we were not allowed to come in contact with him, and we missed him while he had to remain in his own home until he recovered. He could not afford his treatments, so Daddy and Mummy paid for all his medical bills. They also organised a nurse to administer his injections for almost an entire year while supplying him and his family with anything they needed, including paying their rent, until he recovered. Now that we were leaving for Australia, I felt sadness at the thought that I would never see him again.

That morning, the streets were overpopulated with police striding around in khaki summer uniforms – wide-legged and firmly starched shorts, giving their legs the appearance of chicken bones in boots.

'Mary, why do you suppose the police are carrying rifles today? Don't they usually carry a wooden lathi to use on troublemakers? Are we expecting political trouble today?'

Political problems were commonplace. We were accustomed to school being evacuated at short notice during riots, and riding on trams that were set ablaze. Drivers and passengers having to disembark between stops, scurrying away from the trouble.

'It's a scare tactic,' said Mary in a sombre voice.

'Who are they trying to scare?' asked Alison.

'Everyone…' Mary mocked.

Nearer to the airport, police presence intensified. I had never seen such a congregation of police at the airport. Aladdin clutched at his chest as we pulled in near a policeman and stopped at the kerb. My stomach knotted. Mary put her arm around Alison.

'Please, get out here,' Aladdin ordered us out of the car, his voice stern.

'Here?' asked Mary.

'Yes, please, get out quick. Go, go.'

We were unaware what he could see from his rear-view mirror.

In haste, we gathered our belongings and Mary went to open the door when the policeman blocked it. He then fiddled with a rifle, waved the barrel at Aladdin.

'Get out the car,' said the policeman.

Aladdin opened his door in slow motion.

'Hurry up, get out, get out,' the policeman bellowed.

My knotted stomach gurgled. I knew that we had to get out of the country today, with Daddy. Alison's eyes welled; Mary shielded her from the terror by placing her hand over eyes dripping with tears. Aladdin, as if he were a bird ready to take flight, flapped his elbows, with feet firmly planted.

'Where is the sahib who owns this car?'

'We dropped him at his office,' Aladdin outright lied.

The policeman swung the rifle in our direction. I closed my eyes.

'Are these his children?'

'Oh, no,' Aladdin lied again without hesitation. 'This is the first time I am seeing these children. They are family friends going on holidays with their big sister and the sahib is letting them use the car for coming to the airport.'

There was a jolt. I opened my eyes. The policeman must have kicked a tyre or hit it with his gun. Tension was building in my head. Any minute now, it would burst, spurt blood.

The policeman circled the car, then ordered Aladdin, 'Open the boot.'

A few minutes passed, voices raised and fell, the boot was slammed shut and the two men were in my eyesight.

'You better not be lying to me.' The policeman pointed the butt in a forward direction. 'Get out of here.'

'Please, please, I have to drop their luggage,' Aladdin begged.

'Hurry up,' yelled the policeman.

Aladdin hurriedly unloaded suitcases on to the nearby pavement. And the three of us jumped out of the car.

'You can go,' said Mary to Aladdin as if she were talking to a stranger.

And without a goodbye, Aladdin returned to the car and sped away. Alison was crying again and I was filled with dread.

Coolies descended upon us. Mary engaged two of them. They entered the airport ahead of us, carrying luggage on their heads. Mary wiped Alison's face and we braved up, with heads held high, pretending not to notice the police near departures. We followed the coolies, stopping short at a metal barrier – Passengers Only. Our luggage was transferred from heads to a conveyor belt and hands extended for payment.

Hannah was on the other side of the barricade to us, together with Nelson and a man in a navy blue suit who I recognised as Mr Ventura, the travel consultant. He was in conversation with Hannah.

Mary told Alison and me, 'Hurry, go to Hannah.'

I took Alison by the hand and looked back at Mary, who mouthed, 'Please go quickly.'

In the next few months, Hannah would turn eighteen but she already acted as if she was an adult. Mr Ventura handed her a bundle of papers and burgundy-coloured passports. Taking the metal-framed spectacles from his eyes, he wiped and replaced them, brushing his silvery hair back over his head. He rushed past Alison and me without a goodbye. Hannah distributed passports to Nelson and me, together with foolscap sheets of papers. One of them said 'Emigration' at the top.

Hannah asked us to go through the turnstiles to the left behind a wall, pointing in the intended direction. 'Mummy's there and a man who will stamp your papers and passports before we can leave India.'

We turned to wave to Mary.

'Nelson, can you see Mary?' I asked.

He poked his chin forward and looked around. 'No.'

There was a lump in my throat and I recalled that she had kissed us that morning before we got in the car for the airport and asked us not to forget about her in Australia. My heart felt like a heavy lump of dough. Nelson looked as if he had entered a distant place. We hastened to the man behind the wall. I knew then, it would be a very long time before I saw Mary again.

Nelson took control of Alison. Behind the wall, we saw Mummy.

She was carrying her handbag and an overnight bag. Her forehead furrowed with creases. Alison opened her mouth, as if to call out to Mummy, but Nelson stifled the call by covering Alison's mouth with his hand. She cried, but Nelson was correct in his action. At thirteen, Alison was a minor, required to travel on Mummy's passport and we didn't want a scene.

'Where's Daddy?' I asked.

Mummy's voice trembled. 'I don't know.'

'Didn't he come to the airport with you?'

'No, I had to get a taxi here. Daddy had to leave for the airport last night.'

United with our mother, and concerned for our father, we made our way to emigration. The emigration officer wore a dhoti and a kurta with a smart black vest over it. His gold-embossed slip-on shoes, trimmed with red and green leather stripes, curled up at the front with a small bell at the tips.

'Passports and papers please, one person at a time,' he said, eyeballing each of us in turn.

Mummy fanned her face with her emigration papers and kept looking around, sometimes getting up on her toes, peering into the distance.

The emigration officer smiled at the five of us and twirled one corner of his voluptuous moustache. I was the first at the counter.

He opened my papers and passport. 'So, you are going to live in Australia?' he asked.

'Yes, my two older sisters already live there,' I piped up, swollen with pride. Australia, all those years ago was considered the land of milk and honey. Everyone wanted to go there, and we were.

The emigration officer browsed and stamped the white papers, ticking and signing as he went. He lifted a large brass stamp and smacked it down hard in my passport, leaving a wet blue ink stamp in it – 'Departure out of Calcutta'. Then the sound of a second stamp, twice the size of the first, reverberated and sent a shudder down my spine. 'Definite and final'. On a page marked 'visa', he had imprinted, 'Endorsement for Australia', listing down ten items to be completed. Methodically, he filled them in with a fountain pen. I couldn't read them easily upside down but could see that they were dates and numbers. I figured that 'Migrant' was the status on arrival into Australia. Number six had a lot of words printed, so I was up on tiptoes to read upside down – 'residency to be granted on arrival'. The stamps had already sent quivers through me.

He handed the documents back to me. 'You will miss India,' he said.

I saw confirmation of being cleared to leave for Australia. It rocked me. His words somehow felt intimidating but I didn't know why. I wasn't sure if I would miss India or not and looked up at Mummy, but she was smiling the same way she did when she admired the pictures of Queen Elizabeth II that she displayed on her dresser. On the one hand, the excitement of adventure and moving to a new country was uplifting, on the other, where was my father?

At sixteen, I did not understand the full complication of a family immigrating to a new land. It was odd though to be leaving the country forever and not having anyone come to see us off at the airport. My boyfriend had been allowed to spend the previous night with us. I felt unhappy that we would not see each other for a very long time after we had said goodbye to each other earlier that morning. Then, we had pledged to write every day, certain to be reunited when we each finished school in two years' time, him in India and me in Australia. But today, there was a bigger concern.

'Should we wait for Daddy?' Nelson asked Hannah, who had taken control.

'No, Mr Ventura was firm that we should not question things. We are to pass through emigration as quickly as possible and get on the plane.' Hannah gave a fleeting glance at the newly acquired stamps in her passport and closed the document.

Mummy and Alison were the last to see the emigration officer.

Mummy had been using her papers as a makeshift fan. The officer looked at the slightly creased papers and her passport, studied Alison for a few moments and then back to the passport. When he lifted his stamp, I felt an acrid burning in my throat and I had a brief vision of police running through the airport with rifles, lying on their stomachs, combat style, hunting down my father to detain him in the country.

'Come, children, we have to board,' said Mummy in Julie Andrews style, as she hurried the 'Von Trapp' children out of the auditorium.

On board the plane, air hostesses with high cheekbones and glossy pink cheeks, restricted by pink and green embroidered, full-length, slim fitting skirts, took dainty steps, assisting people into seats. Glossy black braids, embellished with purple and white orchids, swung this way and that.

'Good morning, I am Samaden Roy, co-pilot,' the announcement carried through the plane. 'We expect to depart on time.'

I couldn't see Daddy.

Then another announcement. 'We have been detained by security momentarily but expect to have clearance soon.'

I rubbed goosebumps on my arms. Hostesses with manicured hands and pink varnished nails handed out hot towels. Hannah, Nelson and I sat in one row, me in the aisle seat. Hannah climbed onto her seat to check on Alison and Mummy, sitting directly behind her. She had barely turned back to look at them when she jumped down from her seat to alert an air hostess that Mummy had fainted.

Air hostesses were handing out foil miniature bags of peanuts. One delivered a portable oxygen supply to Mummy as if it were peanuts. Affixing a mask to Mummy's face, she shoved the oxygen cylinder in the empty aisle seat beside Mummy. Nelson chewed his nails. Mummy regained consciousness soon after she was given the oxygen.

Hannah reassured the air hostess, 'No need for alarm, she is nervous about flying.'

The air hostess asked Hannah to return to her seat and Hannah squeezed past me.

We were all settled, when men with rifles boarded the plane and took long brisk steps up and down the aisle.

Passengers on the plane bobbed up and down like buoys out at sea. Voices were raised. The air hostesses spoke to some folk and patted them on the arm, smiled and handed around barley sugar wrapped in lemon cellophane.

I looked at Nelson. He had surely gnawed his fingernails down to the quick. Through his window, I saw policemen run around the tarmac, nodding to each other, shaking heads, waving guns. My head pounded, and my heart rattled in my rib cage.

'We will have clearance shortly… Cabin crew, please prepare for take-off,' said Captain Riju Somnath. And the plane's doors closed.

'No!' My lips had formed the words, my father is not here, in anticipation of the sound ejecting at the precise time, but it didn't. My tongue tried to say those words but the breath in my body had been squeezed, wrung out. Drained. Fear clung like a hand to a glove, each fabric finger being pulled over flesh, moulded firmly, snug in place.

Although I was suspended in a space of delirium when an air hostess escorted an unshaven, dark-haired man with fair skin down the aisle, I knew this was no mirage. A man physically weakened, unable to walk upright unaided, was ushered to a seat next to my mother. I saw Mummy's hand reach out to take his. My breath, a tidal river flowing, rushed back into my lungs.

The voice-over said, 'We wish you a pleasant journey. Cabin crew, take your seats.'

Engines roared and it was then that I knew that Daddy would never return to India. I wondered if Mr Ventura was still wiping his brow? Was he in the airport? How had he managed to get Daddy on the plane?

I looked behind to a pale and drawn father. Poor Daddy. Once airborne over Calcutta, I snuggled in my seat, closed my eyes and heard Julie Andrews's powerful voice. 'Climb every mountain…'

Daddy had given Mr Ventura a document and asked him to deliver it to the court as soon as we had departed. It was an apology for his non-attendance in court on a date yet to be set.

In his letter, Daddy told us that he had explained to the court that his family had to leave India when we did to comply with Australian emigration laws and the expiration dates of our visas. Daddy humbly requested the court to understand that he was not being disrespectful in his actions and begged for a pardon.

Daddy could never find anything to criticise in Australia. Everything was praise. He knew that he could never risk a visit to India, but I don't feel he ever regretted his decision to leave.

20

On my return to Australia, an internal fire rages for recognition of my Indian birth, and I waste no time in downloading an application for an OCI (Overseas Citizen of India), which will acknowledge my Indian birth and give me a lifelong visa to India.

An online submission is the only choice to commence a claim for an OCI visa. The information required on the two-page form is collated and checked until I am satisfied that all the requirements have been met. I include a certified sworn affidavit that I have lost my Indian passport, together with a form to renounce my Indian citizenship, and an additional fee for doing so. I pay the fees and submit the form.

Two months to the day later, the Indian visa office notifies me that my Australian passport which specified place of birth – Calcutta, India, is insufficient proof that I was born in India. Neither was a certified copy of my Indian birth certificate nor the baptism certificate collected during a previous trip to India, which also gave my date and place of birth as Calcutta.

Frustrated, I attended the Indian visa office in Sydney in person. Following endless hours waiting, I was called to a counter.

'Show your Indian passport from when you arrived in Australia or your Australian citizenship,' said the woman at the counter, who looked as if she had sucked lemons for breakfast.

'Sorry, I have lost my Indian passport someplace. I have already made that declaration on the document in your possession.'

'Where did you lose it?'

'Somewhere in Australia, I suppose. I don't recall. I have a certified copy of my Australian citizenship certificate and a current Australian passport that gives you my birth city.'

To this authority, it was once again insufficient proof that I had arrived in Australia from India.

'If you can't find your Indian passport, we will want your Indian school leaving certificates.'

'I finished school in Australia. I only have school transfer papers from India.' From my pile of papers, I produce the one in question.

'We cannot give you an OCI. You are not Indian.'

I hear my dead mother concur. I push her voice aside, snatch my passport out of the officer's hand, point out 'Nationality – Australian'.

'I want a permanent OCI visa, which I am entitled to because I was born in India. It is my birthright. I show my Australian passport. Look what this says, "birthplace, Calcutta". My birth and baptism certificates say…'

'That is not sufficient. Besides, just because you were born in India does not make you Indian.'

'What does it make me then?' I query through clenched teeth, and slap my passport down hard onto the counter. I have every possible document that can substantiate my Indian birth. I have a sworn affidavit stating that I lost my Indian passport, and I don't know where it is. Also, that I was born in Calcutta, India. I am a Justice of the Peace, a pillar of my community, with a considerable number of years of voluntary community service. I want to come back to Australia – *I love Australia*. But I am entitled to a permanent visa to visit the country of my birth. I was born in India and I want that recognised.'

'You will need to prove that your family were residents of India,' says the very official woman behind the counter.

'Then tell me what document will prove that – my parents are *dead*. I have given you everything the application asked for.'

A huge sign above the officer's head encourages me to settle – 'Any aggressive behaviour will not be tolerated.' I fully comprehend the need for such a sign to be so boldly displayed in this office.

'Forget it.' I storm off, seething and resolving to go through more humbug and bureaucracy again for my next tourist visa to visit India.

In the lift down to street level, I scream to my dead mother, 'Mummy, you win! I'm not Indian, I never was. You were correct all along.'

Over the next few weeks, I cry every time I think about the blatant robbery of my birthright. I review all my official paperwork again and again in the hope of finding some link to my birth country but there is nothing more I can find to satisfy Indian authorities. I feel the spirituality of India within me and I want recognition. Why am I being denied this right? Will I, can I, in time, get over the fact that it is out of my clutches?

Holding my caul box close to my chest, I say to myself, 'I was born in India, I am Indian.'

I return to India a couple more times in the years that follow and even take Australian groups on tour. Each time on a tourist visa that robs me of my birthright but with an Australian passport, place of birth, Calcutta – accepted.

Months after a trip to India, I visit my youngest sister, Alison, and somehow the topic of my OCI surfaces.

'The Indian government won't give me a permanent visa. I need to prove we were residents there. It costs me emotionally every time I get a tourist visa,' I say.

'What more do they need?' asks Alison.

'I don't think there is anything more I can provide. They wanted my Indian passport, but I don't have one. I have no idea what I did with it after receiving Australian citizenship. Never thought I'd need it again. Becoming Australian and all,' I say, bursting into tears.

Alison hands me a box of tissues and makes tea.

I relax. Accept that it is over. My Indian birth will not be acknowledged. And I need to accept that.

Alison and I see each other at least weekly but the subject of my Indian birth is not raised.

A year later, my Indian birth is still at the back of my mind. Once again at Alison's place, I complain as to how unfair it is that my Indian birth is not recognised.

Alison's face contorts. 'I didn't even have an Indian passport. I was a minor when I left India and my name was only handwritten in Mummy's passport. I didn't even have a photo of me in the passport.'

'Well, you definitely don't even exist by Indian standards.'

An almost amused look of puzzlement flickers over her face. 'I have Mummy's passport. Do you want to try with that?' she asks.

I look through my mother's passport and laugh. 'There is no connection to me in this passport at all. I have documents with Mummy listed as my birth mother, that the authorities won't accept, affidavits… but you know what, I'll give it a try. What have I got to lose? One more round of disappointment?'

Early the next morning, I arrive at the Indian visa office. A ticket machine allocates my place on the waiting list, 104. I squeeze into a single seat between a woman in a sari and one who fidgets with a British passport. A television screen in the waiting room rotates slides – incredible India, the Taj Mahal, temples, saddhus, women with strings of jasmine and marigold entwined around necks. Rings in noses, on fingers, toes. Pots on heads or hips appear, disappear and reappear. I know the very order in which they will come into view. Two hours pass.

My ticket now tatters in my hand, my number flashes, green on a red screen – counter nine.

I place my mother's passport alongside copies of previously lodged paperwork and reference numbers of previous lodgements on the counter and explain the case to the official.

'Will this help?' I don't even make eye contact with the person serving me.

'How do you want to pay the fee?'

I produce my credit card.

A clear plastic zip-lock bag is pulled from under the counter and papers shoved in.

'You will hear by two months' time.'

'Very well, but will my deceased mother's passport be sufficient proof?'

'You have to wait. I am not sure. I am sending it for approval.'
'Surely you can at least tell me if this is correct documentation?'
'No.'
Bureaucratic logic, I think.

Two months to the day following that visit, I am shocked when advised by email that my OCI is ready to collect.
I cradle my caul box. I was born in India, bring me luck.

Once again at the visa office, I think about all the tension and heartache that has led me to this point. When my turn finally arrives, I hand the email to an official.
'You will have to apply again and pay the fee,' growls the same woman that I encountered on previous visits, and I consider myself most unfortunate.
'I will do no such thing. Can't you read?'
I look up at the sign above her counter, Any aggressive behaviour… She walks away and I feel certain that security is being called to haul me out of the building.
Five minutes later, an unlocked plastic security bag is slapped down in front of me and undone. From it, the woman pulls out several sheets of paper and my Australian passport. My eyes fixate on a slim blue booklet the same size as my passport, but considerably slimmer and with the Indian emblem on it.
'Sign here,' says the official, unfolding a document in front of me.
'What am I signing?'
'Collection of OCI.'
I hold the two documents in disbelief as if they are pure gold. I open the blue booklet slowly, carefully. It certifies me as an overseas citizen of India – my passport replicates the *lifelong* visa.
An undone Indian, Mummy smiles on me – lifelong, non-Indian.
I have been validated officially – by my mother, and my mother country.

Author's Note

Between Two Worlds takes its name from the feeling that lay within. I have deep love and respect for Australia and India. I cannot release the bond I have with India, my birthland nor can I love Australia enough for the enormous opportunities it has afforded me. My caul is important to me and remains in my possession.

All events in this memoir are true as I remember them. Some names, including those of my siblings, have been changed to protect their identity.

This is my story and all the information used is derived from documented memories, conversations with family, discussions with people from all walks of life during my travels back to India, and my own learning and experiences. Any errors or misinterpretations are exclusively mine.

Acknowledgements

With respect and gratitude, I acknowledge the Traditional Owners and Custodians of the Dharug lands, waters and seas on which I work and live, paying respects to Elders, past, present and emerging.

Nick Bleszynski, for your belief in my story, recognising my passion, enriching advice and guidance, my sincerest thanks. Without you, this book would not have been completed and for that, I will always be grateful.

Dr Sharon Rundle, I appreciate the valuable time that you took from your busy schedule to copy-edit, and for your consistent and genuine encouragement.

Thank you, members of the Women Writers' Network at Writing NSW, Lilyfield, for your positive critique. In particular, Lyn Macready, Siobhan Colman, Sue Good, Colleen Keating and Decima Wraxall. Also thank you to Margaret Thomason, Glenn Masson and, posthumously, to Dr Patricia Gaut.

Sincere appreciation to Samantha Sirimanne Hyde for your support and friendship. And to Beverley George for introducing us.

I am thankful to Libby Hathorn and Susanne Gervay OAM for your good cheer, Patti Miller for your invaluable masterclasses, and the Society of Women Writers NSW for the many inspiring speakers and workshop presenters.

To my beta readers, Decima Wraxall, Samantha Sirimanne Hyde and Charmaine Hyde, I appreciate your candid observations and reassurances in the memoir's early days.

Emerita Professor Di Yerbury AO and Emerita Professor Elizabeth Webby, I am honoured and humbled by your comments and praise.

My gratitude, Rita Shaw for your keen eye, expertise and assistance.

Sunil Sharma, thank you for taking care of me on my visits to India.

My respect to Swami Sarasvati, Australia, for training me to be a yoga teacher.

Special thanks to my publisher, Stephen Matthews OAM, Ginninderra Press.

My siblings, I hope you enjoy walking down memory lane with me. I appreciate that we will each remember these experiences differently.

Indebtedness to my youngest sister for providing me with our mother's Indian passport.

My deepest love and thanks to my son Daniel for the unforgettable time when we journeyed through India and for your continued support and professional advice. To my daughter Chantal for your counsel and always being there for me. And especially to my husband Gennaro for supporting me in more ways than one and providing me time, space and sustenance when writing and rewriting.

I acknowledge Mrs Gabriel, class teacher, Calcutta, India, and the editorial team of 'Just for Fun'.

JUST FOR FUN

ROUND about the time when the board rooms and the editorial offices of The Statesman were abuzz with ideas and brainwaves about the new Junior Statesman, another magazine for young people—very young people—was being born. At Loreto school, Elliott Road in Calcutta. It was unpretentiously called Just For Fun—the JFF.

The idea for the JFF came from 12-year-old Miss M. Martyr of class 7A, and her friends (also of 7A) decided the idea was worth trying out. It was. Today, nine months and issues later, the JFF is read by all the 40 or so students of class 7A—a JFF club has been formed—and it is a lot of fun.

The editorial staff of five—
THE JUNIOR STATESMAN, JANUARY 13, 1968.

About the Author

Gwen Bitti lives in Sydney, Australia. Born in Kolkata (formerly Calcutta), India, she migrated to Australia when a teenager. She is a business woman, yoga teacher, meditation facilitator and former lecturer for the International Yoga Teachers Association (IYTA). She currently co-ordinates a yoga teachers' support group in Sydney's north-west.

In 2010, together with three other people, Gwen contributed to building a three-storey yoga/community centre in Rimbik, India, as a thank you gift to her birthland.

In 2020, Gwen's short story 'New Life in Kolkata' was selected for an online publication in Agathokakological Aussie Summer, 'a collection of short stories written by people of diverse backgrounds – the objective of the project to celebrate bilateral relationship between India and Australia'. She is a published haiku and tanka poet.

Gwen is a former president of the Society of Women Writers NSW and has supported her local community since the early 1980s. She is currently an active member, volunteer and contributor to the Hornsby Ku-ring-gai community radio station and broadcaster Triple H 100.1FM.

www.ingramcontent.com/pod-product-compliance
Lightning Source LLC
Chambersburg PA
CBHW021100080526
44587CB00010B/315